The Broadview

POCKET GUIDE TO

Citation and Documentation

Second Edition

The Broadview
POCKET GUIDE TO
Citation and Documentation

Second Edition

Maureen Okun and Nora Ruddock

broadview press

BROADVIEW PRESS – www.broadviewpress.com
Peterborough, Ontario, Canada

Founded in 1985, Broadview Press remains a wholly independent publishing house. Broadview's focus is on academic publishing; our titles are accessible to university and college students as well as scholars and general readers. With over 600 titles in print, Broadview has become a leading international publisher in the humanities, with world-wide distribution. Broadview is committed to environmentally responsible publishing and fair business practices.

The interior of this book is printed on 100% recycled paper.

© 2016 Maureen Okun and Nora Ruddock

Library and Archives Canada Cataloguing in Publication

Okun, Maureen, 1961-, author
    The Broadview pocket guide to citation and documentation / Maureen Okun and Nora Ruddock. — Second edition.

Includes bibliographical references.
ISBN 978-1-55481-334-6 (paperback)

        1. Bibliographical citations—Handbooks, manuals, etc.
2. Academic writing—Handbooks, manuals, etc. 3. Report writing—
Handbooks, manuals, etc. 4. Authorship—Style manuals.
I. Ruddock, Nora, author II. Title. III. Title: Pocket guide to
citation and documentation. IV. Title: Citation and documentation.

PN171.F56O48 2016   808.02'7   C2016-905081-5

Broadview Press handles its own distribution in North America
PO Box 1243, Peterborough, Ontario K9J 7H5, Canada
555 Riverwalk Parkway, Tonawanda, NY 14150, USA
Tel: (705) 743-8990; Fax: (705) 743-8353
email: customerservice@broadviewpress.com

Distribution is handled by Eurospan Group in the UK, Europe, Central Asia, Middle East, Africa, India, Southeast Asia, Central America, South America, and the Caribbean. Distribution is handled by Footprint Books in Australia and New Zealand.

Broadview Press acknowledges the financial support
of the Government of Canada through the
Canada Book Fund for our publishing activities.

Design and typeset by Eileen Eckert
Cover design by Lisa Brawn

PRINTED IN CANADA

CONTENTS

Contents

Contents

Contents

◉ DOCUMENTATION AND RESEARCH

Writers have a variety of reasons for including the results of research in their essays. Outside sources can help support or clarify authors' points, or can provide opposing arguments against which authors can make their own case. Sources are also useful in showing where a paper can be located in the wider conversation among writers engaged by the same subject. At the very least, including source material is one way writers can show that they are acquainted with the latest thinking on their topics.

Whatever the reasons for incorporating research into their essays, good writers are careful in how they do so, making sure to document their sources accurately and completely. This is, first of all, a service to readers who would like to embark on a fuller investigation into the topic of a paper by looking up its sources themselves; every academic citation system gives readers all the information they need to access original source material. But it is also critical that there be complete clarity about which parts of an essay are the author's and which parts come from elsewhere. To allow any blurriness on this question is to be dishonest, to engage in a kind of cheating, in fact—known as plagiarism.

○ *Avoiding Plagiarism—and Choosing When and What to Quote*

Most people understand that taking someone else's writing and passing it off as one's own is intellectual thievery. But it is important to be aware that you may commit plagiarism even if you do not use precisely the same words another person wrote in precisely the same order. For instance, here is an actual example of plagiarism. *Globe and Mail* newspaper columnist Margaret Wente borrowed material for one of her columns from a number of works, including an article by Dan Gardner that had appeared the previous year in another newspaper (the *Ottawa Citizen*) and a book by Robert Paarlberg called *Starved for Science* (which was the subject of Gardner's article). The similarities were brought to light by media commentator Carol Wainio, who presented a series of parallel passages, including the following, on her blog *Media Culpa* (the fonts are Wainio's—simple bold is for direct copying; the bold + italics is for "near copying"):

> Gardner: ***Many NGOs working in Africa in the area of development and the environment have been advocating against the modernization of traditional farming practices***, Paarlberg says. "**They believe that traditional farming in Africa incorporates indigenous knowledge that shouldn't be replaced by science-based knowledge introduced from the outside.** They encourage Africa to stay away from fertilizers, and be certified as organic instead. And in the case of genetic engineering, they warn African governments against making these technologies available to farmers."

Wente: ***Yet, many NGOs working in Africa have tenaciously fought the modernization of traditional farming practices.* They believe traditional farming in Africa incorporates indigenous knowledge that shouldn't be replaced by science-based knowledge introduced from the outside.** As Prof. Paarlberg writes, "They encourage African farmers to stay away from fertilizers and be certified organic instead. And they warn African governments to stay away from genetic engineering."

Wente does not always use exactly the same words as her sources, but no one reading the passages can doubt that one writer is appropriating the phrasings of the others. Additionally, where Wente *does* quote Paarlberg directly, the quotation is lifted from Gardner's article and should be identified as such.

The penalties for such practices are not trivial; Wente was publicly reprimanded by her employer, and the CBC radio program *Q* removed her from its media panel. Other reporters have been, justifiably, fired under similar circumstances. At most colleges and universities, students are likely to receive a zero if they are caught plagiarizing—and they may be expelled from the institution. It's important to be aware, too, that penalties for plagiarism make no allowance for intent; it is no defense that a writer took someone else's words "by mistake" rather than intentionally.

How, then, can you be sure to avoid plagiarism? First of all, be extremely careful in your note-taking, so as to make it impossible to imagine, a few days later, that words you have jotted down from somewhere else are your own. This is why notes need to be in a separate file or book from your own ideas. (In her *Globe and Mail* column responding to the plagiarism charges, Wente, in fact, claimed that she had accidentally mixed a quotation into her own ideas.) If your note-taking is reliable, then you will know which words need to be credited. One way to rewrite the passage above would simply be to remove the material taken from Gardner and to credit Paarlberg by quoting him directly, if you were able to access his book and could do so: "As Robert Paarlberg has argued in his book *Starved for Science*, many NGOs 'believe that traditional farming in Africa incorporates indigenous knowledge that shouldn't be replaced by science-based knowledge introduced from the outside.'" You would, of course, look up and provide the page number as well.

You may notice that the quoted material is a statement of opinion rather than fact—controversial views are being given, but without any evidence provided to back them up—so a careful reader would wonder whether NGOs are really as anti-science as the quotation suggests, or whether the writer hasn't done enough research on the debate. If you were to make an assertion like this in a paper of your own it would not be enough just to quote Paarlberg; you would need to do much more research and find information to support or deny your claim. If you are including quotations in an essay, the best sources to quote are not necessarily those which express opinions that mirror the ones you are putting forward. In a case such as this, for example, the argument would have been much more persuasive if Wente had quoted an official statement from one of the NGOs she was attacking. If her article had quoted a source making this specific case against "science-based knowledge" and then argued directly against that source's argument, Wente's own position would have been strengthened. Quoting many such sources would provide proof that the article's characterization of the position of NGOs was factually accurate.

Whenever you do quote someone else, it's important to cite the source. But do you need a citation for everything that did not come from your own knowledge? Not necessarily. Citations are usually unnecessary when you are touching on common knowledge (provided it is, in fact, common knowledge, and provided your instructor has not asked you to do otherwise). If you refer to the chemical composition of water, or the date when penicillin was discovered, you are unlikely to need to provide any citation, even if you used a source to find the information, since such facts are generally available and uncontroversial. (Make sure, however, to check any "common knowledge" with several reputable sources; if your information is incorrect, it reflects poorly on you, especially if you have not cited your source.) If you have any doubts about whether something is common knowledge or not, cite it; over-cautiousness is not a serious problem, but plagiarism always is.

O *Citation and Documentation*

Citing sources is fundamental to writing a good research paper, but no matter how diligent you are in making your acknowledgements, your paper will not be taken seriously unless its documentation is formatted according to an appropriate and accepted referencing style. For the sake of consistency, each academic discipline has adopted a particular system of referencing as its standard, which those writing in that discipline are expected to follow. *The Broad-*

view Pocket Guide to Citation and Documentation outlines the four most common of these systems. Almost all of the humanities use the documentation guidelines developed by the Modern Language Association (MLA), a notable exception being history, which tends to prefer those of the *Chicago Manual of Style* (Chicago Style). The social and some health sciences typically follow the style rules of the American Psychological Association (APA), while the basic sciences most commonly use the referencing systems of the Council of Science Editors (CSE). Each of these styles is exacting and comprehensive in its formatting rules; following with precision the one recommended for a given paper's discipline is one of a responsible research writer's duties. Details of these systems are in the pages that follow.

As important as documentation is to a well-written paper, by itself it is not always enough. Writers must also be attentive to the ways in which they integrate borrowed material into their essays.

O *Incorporating Sources*

There are three main ways of working source material into a paper: summarizing, paraphrasing, and quoting directly. In order to avoid plagiarism, care must be taken with all three kinds of borrowing, both in the way they are handled and in their referencing. In what follows, a passage from page 102 of a book by Terrence W. Deacon (*The Symbolic Species: The Co-Evolution of Language and the Brain*, New York: Norton, 1997) serves as the source for a sample summary, paraphrase, and quotation. The examples feature the MLA style of in-text parenthetical citations, but the requirements for presenting the source material are the same for all academic referencing systems. For a similar discussion with a focus on APA style, see Incorporating Sources in APA Style (starting on page 91).

original source   Over the last few decades language researchers seem to have reached a consensus that language is an innate ability, and that only a significant contribution from innate knowledge can explain our ability to learn such a complex communication system. Without question, children enter the world predisposed to learn human languages. All normal children, raised in normal social environments, inevitably learn their local language, whereas other species, even when raised and taught in this same environment, do not. This demonstrates that human brains come into the world specially equipped for this function.

O *Summarizing*

An honest and competent summary, whether of a passage or an entire book, must not only represent the source accurately but also use original wording and include a citation. It is a common misconception that only quotations need to be acknowledged as borrowings in the body of an essay. In fact, without a citation, even a fairly worded summary or paraphrase is an act of plagiarism. The first example below is faulty on two counts: it borrows wording (underlined) from the source, and it has no parenthetical reference.

needs checking   <u>Researchers</u> agree that language learning is <u>innate, and that only innate knowledge can explain</u> how we are able <u>to learn</u> a <u>system</u> of <u>communication</u> that is so <u>complex</u>. <u>Normal children raised in normal</u> ways will always <u>learn their local language, whereas other species do not, even when taught</u> human language and exposed to the <u>same environment</u>.

The next example correctly avoids the wording of the source passage, and a signal phrase and parenthetical citation note the author and page number.

revised   As Terrence W. Deacon notes, there is now wide agreement among linguists that the ease with which human children acquire their native tongues, under the conditions of a normal childhood, demonstrates an inborn capacity for language that is not shared by any other animals, not even those who are reared in comparable ways and given human language training (102).

○ *Paraphrasing*

Whereas a summary is a shorter version of its original, a paraphrase tends to be about the same length. However, paraphrases, just like summaries, must reflect their sources accurately, must use original wording, and must include a citation. Even though it is properly cited, the paraphrase of the first sentence of the Deacon passage, below, falls short by being too close to the wording of the original (underlined).

needs checking   <u>Researchers</u> in <u>language</u> have come to <u>a consen-</u>
<u>sus</u> in the past <u>few decades</u> that the acquisition
of language is <u>innate</u>; such <u>contributions</u> <u>from</u>
<u>knowledge</u> <u>contribute significantly</u> to <u>our abil-</u>
<u>ity</u> to master <u>such a complex system</u> of <u>com-</u>
<u>munication</u> (Deacon 102).

Simply substituting synonyms for the words and phrases
of the source, however, is not enough to avoid plagiarism.
Despite its original wording, the next example also fails but
for a very different reason: it follows the original's sentence
structure too closely, as illustrated in the interpolated copy
below it.

needs checking   Recently, linguists appear to have come to an
agreement that speaking is an inborn skill,
and that nothing but a substantial input from
inborn cognition can account for the human
capacity to acquire such a complicated means
of expression (Deacon 102).

Recently (*over the last few decades*), linguists
(*language researchers*) appear to have come to
an agreement (*seem to have reached a consensus*)
that speaking is an inborn skill (*that language is
an innate ability*), and that nothing but a substantial input (*and that only a significant contribution*) from inborn cognition (*from innate
knowledge*) can account for the human capacity
(*can explain our ability*) to acquire such a complicated means of expression (*to learn such a
complex communication system*) (Deacon 102).

What follows is a good paraphrase of the passage's opening sentence; this paraphrase captures the sense of the original without echoing the details and shape of its language.

> *revised*   Linguists now broadly agree that children are born with the ability to learn language; in fact, the human capacity to acquire such a difficult skill cannot easily be accounted for in any other way (Deacon 102).

O *Quoting Directly*

Unlike paraphrases and summaries, direct quotations must use the exact wording of the original. Because they involve importing outside words, quotations pose unique challenges. Quote too frequently, and you risk making your readers wonder why they are not reading your sources instead of your paper. Your essay should present something you want to say—informed and supported by properly documented sources, but forming a contribution that is yours alone. To that end, use secondary material to help you build a strong framework for your work, not to replace it. Quote sparingly, therefore; use your sources' exact wording only when it is important or particularly memorable.

To avoid misrepresenting your sources, be sure to quote accurately, and to avoid plagiarism, take care to indicate quotations as quotations, and cite them properly. Below are two problematic quotations. The first does not show which words come directly from the source.

needs checking   Terrence W. Deacon maintains that children enter the world predisposed to learn human languages (102).

The second quotation fails to identify the source at all.

needs checking   Linguists believe that "children enter the world predisposed to learn human languages."

The next example corrects both problems by naming the source and indicating clearly which words come directly from it.

revised   Terrence W. Deacon maintains that "children enter the world predisposed to learn human languages" (102).

◎ FORMATTING QUOTATIONS

There are two ways to signal an exact borrowing: by enclosing it in double quotation marks and by indenting it as a block of text. Which you should choose depends on the length and genre of the quotation and the style guide you are following.

⊙ Short Prose Quotations

What counts as a short prose quotation differs among the various reference guides. In MLA style, "short" means up to four lines; in APA, up to forty words; and in Chicago Style, up to one hundred words. All the guides agree, however, that short quotations must be enclosed in double quotation marks, as in the examples below.

Short quotation, full sentence:
According to Terrence W. Deacon, linguists agree that a human child's capacity to acquire language is inborn: "Without question, children enter the world predisposed to learn human languages" (102).

Short quotation, partial sentence:
According to Terrence W. Deacon, linguists agree that human "children enter the world predisposed to learn human languages" (102).

Documentation and Research

☉ Long Prose Quotations

Longer prose quotations should be double-spaced and indented, as a block, one tab space from the left margin. Do not include quotation marks; the indentation indicates that the words come exactly from the source. Note that indented quotations are often introduced with a full sentence followed by a colon.

> Terrence W. Deacon, like most other linguists, believes that human beings are born with a unique cognitive capacity:
>
> > Without question, children enter the world predisposed to learn human languages. All normal children, raised in normal social environments, inevitably learn their local language, whereas other species, even when raised and taught in this same environment, do not. This demonstrates that human brains come into the world specially equipped for this function. (102)

⊙ Verse Quotations

Quoting from verse is a special case. Poetry quotations of three or fewer lines (MLA) may be integrated into your paragraph and enclosed in double quotation marks, with lines separated by a forward slash with a space on either side of it, as in the example below.

> Pope's "Epistle II. To a Lady," in its vivid portrayal of wasted lives, sharply criticizes the social values that render older women superfluous objects of contempt: "Still round and round the Ghosts of Beauty glide, / And haunt the places where their Honor dy'd" (lines 241–42).

If your quotation of three or fewer lines includes a stanza break, MLA style requires you to mark the break by inserting two forward slashes (//), with spaces on either side of them.

> The speaker in "Ode to a Nightingale" seeks, in various ways, to free himself from human consciousness, leaving suffering behind. Keats uses alliteration and repetition to mimic the gradual dissolution of self, the process of intoxication or death: "That I might drink, and leave the world unseen, / And with thee fade away into the forest dim: // Fade far away, dissolve, and quite forget" (lines 19–21).

Poetry quotations of more than three lines in MLA, or two or more lines in Chicago Style, should be, like long prose quotations, indented and set off in a block from your main text. Arrange the lines just as they appear in the original.

The ending of Margaret Avison's "September Street" moves from the decaying, discordant city toward a glimpse of an outer/inner infinitude:

> On the yellow porch
> one sits, not reading headlines; the old eyes
> read far out into the mild
> air, runes.
> See. There: a stray sea-gull. (lines 20–24)

⊙ Quotations within Quotations

You may sometimes find, within the original passage you wish to quote, words already enclosed in double quotation marks. If your quotation is short, enclose it all in double quotation marks, and use single quotation marks for the embedded quotation.

> Terrence W. Deacon is firm in maintaining that human language differs from other communication systems in kind rather than degree: "Of no other natural form of communication is it legitimate to say that 'language is a more complicated version of that'" (44).

If your quotation is long, keep the double quotation marks of the original.

> Terrence W. Deacon is firm in maintaining that human language differs from other communication systems in kind rather than degree:
>
> > Of no other natural form of communication is it legitimate to say that "language is a more complicated version of that." It is just as misleading to

call other species' communication systems *simple* languages as it is to call them languages. In addition to asserting that a Procrustean mapping of one to the other is possible, the analogy ignores the sophistication and power of animals' non-linguistic communication, whose capabilities may also be without language parallels. (44)

⊙ Adding to or Deleting from a Quotation

While it is important to use the original's exact wording in a quotation, it is allowable to modify a quotation somewhat, as long as the changes are clearly indicated and do not distort the meaning of the original.

Ⓞ *Using square brackets to add to a quotation*

You may want to add to a quotation in order to clarify what would otherwise be puzzling or ambiguous to someone who does not know its context; in that case, put whatever you add in square brackets.

Terrence W. Deacon writes that children are born "specially equipped for this [language] function" (102).

Ⓞ *Using an ellipsis to delete from a quotation*

If you would like to streamline a quotation by omitting anything unnecessary to your point, insert an ellipsis (three spaced dots) to show that you've left material out.

When the quotation looks like a complete sentence but is actually part of a longer sentence, you should provide an ellipsis to show that there is more to the original than you are using.

> Terrence W. Deacon says that ". . . children enter the world predisposed to learn human languages" (102).

Note that if the quotation is clearly a partial sentence, ellipses aren't necessary.

> Terrence W. Deacon writes that children are born "specially equipped" to learn human language (102).

When the omitted material runs over a sentence boundary or constitutes a whole sentence or more, insert a period plus an ellipsis.

> Terrence W. Deacon, like most other linguists, believes that human children are born with a unique ability to acquire their native language: "Without question, children enter the world predisposed to learn human languages. . . . [H]uman brains come into the world specially equipped for this function" (102).

Be sparing in modifying quotations; it is all right to have one or two altered quotations in a paper, but if you find yourself changing quotations often, or adding to and omitting from one quotation more than once, reconsider quoting at all. A paraphrase or summary is very often a more effective choice.

⊙ Integrating Quotations

Quotations must be worked smoothly and grammatically into your sentences and paragraphs. Always, of course, mark quotations as such, but for the purpose of integrating them into your writing, treat them as if they were your own words. The boundary between what you say and what your source says should be grammatically seamless.

needs checking   Terrence W. Deacon points out, "whereas other species, even when raised and taught in this same environment, do not" (102).

revised   According to Terrence W. Deacon, while human children brought up under normal conditions acquire the language they are exposed to, "other species, even when raised and taught in this same environment, do not" (102).

O *Avoiding "dumped" quotations*

Integrating quotations well also means providing a context for them. Don't merely drop them into your paper or string them together like beads on a necklace; make sure to introduce them by noting where the material comes from and how it connects to whatever point you are making.

needs checking   For many years, linguists have studied how human children acquire language. "Without question, children enter the world predisposed to learn human language" (Deacon 102).

revised   Most linguists studying how human children acquire language have come to share the conclusion articulated here by Terrence W. Deacon: "Without question, children enter the world predisposed to learn human language" (102).

needs checking   "Without question, children enter the world predisposed to learn human language" (Deacon 102). "There is . . . something special about human brains that enables us to do with ease what no other species can do even minimally without intense effort and remarkably insightful training" (Deacon 103).

revised   Terrence W. Deacon bases his claim that we "enter the world predisposed to learn human language" on the fact that very young humans can "do with ease what no other species can do even minimally without intense effort and remarkably insightful training" (102–03).

O *Signal Phrases*

To leave no doubt in your readers' minds about which parts of your essay are yours and which come from elsewhere, identify the sources of your summaries, paraphrases, and quotations with signal phrases, as in the following examples.

- As Carter and Rosenthal have demonstrated, . . .
- In the words of one researcher, . . .
- In his most recent book McGann advances the view that, as he puts it, . . .
- As Nussbaum observes, . . .
- Kendal suggests that . . .
- Freschi and other scholars have rejected these claims, arguing that . . .
- Morgan has emphasized this point in her recent research: . . .
- As Sacks puts it, . . .

- To be sure, Mtele allows that . . .
- In his later novels Hardy takes a bleaker view, frequently suggesting that . . .

In order to help establish your paper's credibility, you may also find it useful at times to include in a signal phrase information that shows why readers should take the source seriously, as in the following example:

> In her landmark work, biologist and conservationist Rachel Carson warns that . . .

Here, the signal phrase mentions the author's professional credentials; it also points out the importance of her book, which is appropriate to do in the case of a work as famous as Carson's *Silent Spring*.

Below is a fuller list of words and expressions that may be useful in the crafting of signal phrases:

according to _____,	endorses
acknowledges	finds
adds	grants
admits	illustrates
advances	implies
agrees	in the view of _____,
allows	in the words of _____,
argues	insists
asserts	intimates
attests	notes
believes	observes
claims	points out
comments	puts it
compares	reasons
concludes	refutes
confirms	rejects
contends	reports
declares	responds
demonstrates	suggests
denies	takes issue with
disputes	thinks
emphasizes	writes

MLA Style

◎ MLA Style

"MLA style" refers to the referencing guidelines of the Modern Language Association, which are favoured by many disciplines in the humanities. The main components of the MLA system are in-text author-page number citations for the body of an essay, and a bibliography giving publication details—the list of "Works Cited"—at the end of it.

This section outlines the key points of MLA style. A full-length sample essay appears at the end of this book, and additional sample essays can be found on the Broadview website; go to sites.broadviewpress.com/writing. Consult the *MLA Handbook* (8th edition, 2016) if you have questions not answered here; you may also find answers at the website of the MLA, www.mla.org, where updates and answers to frequently asked questions are posted.

MLA Style

O *About In-Text Citations*

1. in-text citations: Under the MLA system a quotation or specific reference to another work is followed by a parenthetical page reference:

- Bonnycastle refers to "the true and lively spirit of opposition" with which Marxist literary criticism invigorates the discipline (204).

The work is then listed under "Works Cited" at the end of the essay:

- Bonnycastle, Stephen. *In Search of Authority: An Introductory Guide to Literary Theory.* 3rd ed., Broadview Press, 2007.

  (See below for information about the "Works Cited" list.)

2. no signal phrase (or author not named in signal phrase): If the context does not make it clear who the author is, that information must be added to the in-text citation. Note that no comma separates the name of the author from the page number.

- Even in recent years some have continued to believe that Marxist literary criticism invigorates the discipline with a "true and lively spirit of opposition" (Bonnycastle 204).

3. placing of in-text citations: Place in-text citations at the ends of clauses or sentences in order to keep disruption of your writing to a minimum. The citation comes before the period or comma in the surrounding sentence. (If the quotation ends with punctuation other than a period or comma, then this should precede the end of the quotation, and a period or comma should still follow the in-text citation.)

- Ricks refuted this point early on (16), but the claim has continued to be made in recent years.
- In "The Windhover," on the other hand, Hopkins bubbles over; "the mastery of the thing!" (8), he enthuses when he thinks of a bird, exclaiming shortly thereafter, "O my chevalier!" (10).

When a cited quotation is set off from the text, however, the in-text citation should be placed after the concluding punctuation.

- Muriel Jaeger draws on the following anecdote in discussing the resistance of many wealthy Victorians to the idea of widespread education for the poor:

  > In a mischievous mood, Henry Brougham once told [some well-off acquaintances who were] showing perturbation about the likely results of educating the "lower orders" that they could maintain their superiority by working harder themselves. (105)

4. in-text citation when text is in parentheses: If an in-text citation occurs within text in parentheses, square brackets are used for the reference.

- The development of a mass literary culture (or a "print culture," to use Williams's expression [88]) took several hundred years in Britain.

5. page number unavailable: Many Web sources lack page numbers. If your source has no page or section numbers, no number should be given in your citation. Do not count paragraphs yourself, as the version you are using may differ from others.

- In a recent Web posting a leading critic has clearly implied that he finds such an approach objectionable (Bhabha).

If the source gives explicit paragraph or section numbers, as many Websites do, cite the appropriate abbreviation, followed by the number.

- Early in the novel, Austen makes clear that the "business" of Mrs. Bennet's life is "to get her daughters married" (ch. 1).

- In "The American Scholar" Emerson asserts that America's "long apprenticeship to the learning of other lands" is drawing to a close (par. 7).

Note that (as is not the case with page numbers), MLA style requires a comma between author and paragraph or section numbers in a citation.

- Early in the novel, Mrs. Bennet makes it clear that her sole business in life is "to get her daughters married" (Austen, ch. 1).

6. one page or less: If a source is one page long or less, it is advisable to still provide the page number (though MLA does not require this).

- In his *Chicago Tribune* review, Bosley calls the novel's prose "excruciating" (1).

7. **multiple authors**: If there are two authors, both authors should be named either in the signal phrase or in the in-text citation, connected by *and*.

- Chambliss and Best argue that the importance of this novel is primarily historical (233).

- Two distinguished scholars have recently argued that the importance of this novel is primarily historical (Chambliss and Best 233).

If there are three or more authors, include only the first author's name in the in-text citation, followed by *et al.*, short for the Latin *et alii*, meaning *and others*.

- Meaning is not simply there in the text, but in the complex relationships between the text, the reader, and the Medieval world (Black et al. xxxvi).

8. **corporate author**: The relevant organization or the title of the piece should be included in the in-text citation if neither is included in the body of your text; make sure enough information is provided for readers to find the correct entry in your Works Cited list. Shorten a long title to avoid awkwardness, but take care that the shortened version begins with the same word as the corresponding entry in "Works Cited" so that readers can move easily from the citation to the bibliographic information. For example, *Comparative Indo-European Linguistics: An Introduction* should be shortened to *Comparative Indo-European* rather than *Indo-European Linguistics*. The first two examples below cite unsigned newspaper or encyclopedia articles; the last is a corporate author in-text citation.

- As *The New York Times* reported in one of its several December 2 articles on the Florida recount, Vice-President Gore looked tired and strained as he answered questions ("Gore Press Conference" A16).

- In the 1990s Sao Paulo began to rapidly overtake Mexico City as the world's most polluted city ("Air Pollution" 21).

- There are a number of organizations mandated "to foster the production and enjoyment of the arts in Canada" (Canada Council for the Arts 2).

9. more than one work by the same author cited: If you include more than one work by the same author in your list of Works Cited, you must make clear which work is being cited each time. This may be done either by mentioning the work in a signal phrase or by including in the citation a short version of the title.

- In *The House of Mirth*, for example, Wharton writes of love as keeping Lily and Selden "from atrophy and extinction" (282).

- Wharton sees love as possessing the power to keep humans "from atrophy and extinction" (*House of Mirth* 282).

- Love, as we learn from the experience of Lily and Selden, possesses the power to keep humans "from atrophy and extinction" (Wharton, *House of Mirth* 282).

MLA Style

10. multi-volume works: Note, by number, the volume you are referring to, followed by a colon and a space, before noting the page number. Use the abbreviation "vol." when citing an entire volume.

- Towards the end of *In Darkest Africa* Stanley refers to the Victoria Falls (2: 387).

- In contrast with those of the medieval period, Renaissance artworks show an increasing concern with depicting the material world and less and less of an interest in metaphysical symbolism (Hauser, vol. 2).

11. two or more authors with the same last name: If the Works Cited list includes two or more authors with the same last name, the in-text citation should supply both first initials and last names, or, if the first initials are also the same, the full first and last names:

- One of the leading economists of the time advocated wage and price controls (Harry Johnston 197).

- One of the leading economists of the time advocated wage and price controls (H. Johnston 197).

12. indirect quotations: When an original source is not available but is referred to by another source, the in-text citation includes *qtd. in* (an abbreviation of *quoted in*) and a reference to the second source. In the example below, Casewell is quoted by Bouvier; the in-text citation directs readers to an entry in Works Cited for the Bouvier work.

- Casewell considers Lambert's position to be "outrageously arrogant" (qtd. in Bouvier 59).

13. short poems: For short poems, cite line numbers rather than page numbers.

- In "Dover Beach" Arnold hears the pebbles in the waves bring the "eternal note of sadness in" (line 14).

If you are citing the same poem repeatedly, use just the numbers for subsequent references.

- The world, in Arnold's view, has "really neither joy, nor love, nor light" (33).

14. longer poems: For longer poems with parts, cite the part (or section, or "book") as well as the line (where available). Use Arabic numerals, and use a period for separation.

- In "Ode: Intimations of Immortality" Wordsworth calls human birth "but a sleep and a forgetting" (5.1).

15. novels or short stories: When a work of prose fiction has chapters or numbered divisions the citation should include first the page number, and then book, chapter, and section numbers as applicable. (These can be very useful in helping readers of a different edition to locate the passage you are citing.) Arabic numerals should be used. A semicolon should be used to separate the page number from the other information.

- When Joseph and Fanny are by themselves, they immediately express their affection for each other, or, as Fielding puts it, "solace themselves" with "amorous discourse" (151; ch. 26).

- In *Tender Is the Night* Dick's ambition does not quite crowd out the desire for love: "He wanted to be loved too, if he could fit it in" (133; bk. 2, ch. 4).

MLA Style

16. plays: Almost all plays are divided into acts and/or scenes. For plays that do not include line numbering throughout, cite the page number in the edition you have been using, followed by act and/or scene numbers as applicable:

- As Angie and Joyce begin drinking together Angie pronounces the occasion "better than Christmas" (72; act 3).

- Near the conclusion of Inchbald's *Wives as They Were* Bronzely declares that he has been "made to think with reverence on the matrimonial compact" (62; act 5, sc. 4).

For plays written entirely or largely in verse, where line numbers are typically provided throughout, you should omit the reference to page number in the citation. Instead, cite the act, scene, and line numbers, using Arabic numerals. For a Shakespeare play, if the title isn't clear from the introduction to a quotation, an abbreviation of the title may also be used. The in-text citation below is for Shakespeare's *The Merchant of Venice*, Act 2, Scene 3, lines 2–4:

- Jessica clearly has some fondness for Launcelot: "Our house is hell, and thou, a merry devil, / Dost rob it of some taste of tediousness. / But fare thee well; there is a ducat for thee" (*MV* 2.3.2–4).

17. works without page numbers: If you are citing literary texts where you have consulted editions from other sources (on the Web or in an ebook, for instance), the principles are exactly the same, except that you need not cite page numbers. For example, if the online Gutenberg edition of Fielding's *Joseph Andrews* were being cited, the citation would be as follows:

- When Joseph and Fanny are by themselves, they immediately express their affection for each other, or, as Fielding puts it, "solace themselves" with "amorous discourse" (ch. 26).

Students should be cautioned that online editions of literary texts are often unreliable. Typically there are far more typos and other errors in online versions of literary texts than there are in print versions, and such things as the layout of poems are also frequently incorrect. It is often possible to exercise judgement about such matters, however. If, for example, you are not required to base your essay on a particular copy of a Thomas Hardy poem but may find your own, you will be far better off using the text you will find on the Representative Poetry Online site run out of the University of Toronto than you will using a text you might find on a "World's Finest Love Poems" site.

18. sacred texts: The Bible and other sacred texts that are available in many editions should be cited in a way that enables the reader to check the reference in any edition. For the Bible, book, chapter, and verse should all be cited, using periods for separation. The reference below is to Genesis, chapter 2, verse 1.

- According to the Judeo-Christian story of creation, at the end of the sixth day "the heavens and the earth were finished" (Gen. 2.1).

19. works in an anthology or book of readings: In the in-text citation for a work in an anthology, use the name of the author of the work, not that of the editor of the anthology. The page number, however, should be that found in the anthology. The following citation refers to an article by Frederic W. Gleach in an anthology edited by Jennifer Brown and Elizabeth Vibert.

- One of the essays in Brown and Vibert's collection argues that we should rethink the Pocahontas myth (Gleach 48).

In your list of Works Cited, this work should be alphabetized under Gleach, the author of the piece you have consulted, not under Brown. If you cite another work by a different author from the same anthology or book of readings, that should appear as a separate entry in your list of Works Cited—again, alphabetized under the author's name.

20. tweets: Cite tweets by giving the author's name in your text rather than in an in-text citation.

- Jack Welch quickly lost credibility when he tweeted that the US Bureau of Labor had manipulated monthly unemployment rate statistics in order to boost the post-debate Obama campaign: "Unbelievable job numbers..these Chicago guys will do anything..can't debate so change numbers."

○ *About Works Cited; MLA Core Elements*

The Works Cited list in MLA style is an alphabetized list at the end of the essay (or article or book). The entire list, like the main part of the essay, should be double-spaced throughout, and each entry should be given a hanging indent: the first line is flush with the left-hand margin, and each subsequent line is indented one tab space.

The Works Cited list should include information about all the sources you have cited. Do not include works that you consulted but did not cite in the body of your text.

MLA style provides a set of citation guidelines that the writer follows and adapts, regardless of whether the source being cited is print, digital, audio, visual, or any other form of media. All sources share what the MLA call "Core Elements," and these, listed in order, create the citation for all your entries: Author, Title of Source, Title of Container (larger whole), Other Contributors, Version, Number, Publisher, Publication Date, and Location. Each element is followed by the punctuation marks shown in the table below, unless it is the last element, which should always close with a period. (There are a few exceptions to this rule, which are outlined below.) Most sources don't have all the elements (some don't have an author, for example, or a version, or a location); if you find that this is the case, omit the element and move on to the next.

The table can function as a guide when creating citations. Once you have found all the publication details for your source, place them in order and punctuate according to the table, leaving out any elements for which you don't have information.

1. Author.
2. Title of source.
3. Title of container,
4. Other contributors,
5. Version,
6. Number,
7. Publisher,
8. Publication Date,
9. Location.

In the sections below, you will discover how to identify the core elements of MLA style and how to use them across media. For a list of examples, please see pages 68 to 84.

Author

This element begins your citation. For a **single author**, list the author's last name first, followed by a comma, and then the author's first name or initials (use whatever appears on the work's title page or copyright page), followed by a period.

Graham, Jorie. *From the New World*. Ecco, 2015.

McKerlie, Dennis. *Justice between the Young and the Old*. Oxford UP, 2013.

If a source has **two authors**, the first author's name should appear with the last name first, followed by a comma and *and*. Note also that the authors' names should appear in the order they are listed; sometimes this is not alphabetical.

> Rectenwald, Michael, and Lisa Carl. *Academic Writing, Real World Topics.* Broadview Press, 2015.

If there are **three or more authors**, include only the first author's name, reversed, followed by a comma and *et al.* (the abbreviation of the Latin *et alii*, meaning *and others*).

> Blais, Andre, et al. *Anatomy of a Liberal Victory.* Broadview Press, 2002.

Sources that are **edited** rather than authored are usually cited in a similar way; add "editor" or "editors" after the name(s) and before the title.

> Renker, Elizabeth, editor. *Poems: A Concise Anthology.* Broadview Press, 2016.

When referring to an edited version of a work written by another author or authors, list the editor(s) after the title, in the Other Contributors element.

> Trollope, Anthony. *The Eustace Diamonds.* 1873. Edited by Stephen Gill and John Sutherland, Penguin, 1986.

Authors can be organizations, institutions, associations, or government agencies ("corporate authors"). If a work has been issued by a **corporate author** and no author is identified, the entry should be listed by the name of the organization that produced it.

> Ontario, Ministry of Natural Resources. *Achieving Balance: Ontario's Long-Term Energy Plan.* Queen's Printer for Ontario, 2016, www.energy.gov.on.ca /en/ltep/achieving-balance-ontarios-long-term -energy-plan. Accessed 10 May 2016.

If the work is published by the same organization that is the corporate author, skip the author element and list only the publisher. The citation will begin with the source title.

> *2014 Annual Report.* Broadview Press, 2015.

> "History of the Arms and Great Seal of the Common-wealth of Massachusetts." Commonwealth of Massachusetts, www.sec.state.ma.us/pre/presea/sealhis/htm. Accessed 9 May 2016.

> "Our Mandate." Art Gallery of Ontario, www.ago.net/mandate. Accessed 10 May 2016.

Works with an **anonymous author** should be alphabetized by title, omitting the author element.

> *Sir Gawain and the Green Knight.* Edited by Paul Battles, Broadview Press, 2012.

Works under a **pseudonym** should appear with the pseudonym in place of the author's name. Online usernames are copied out exactly as they appear on the screen.

> @newyorker. "With the resignation of Turkey's Prime Minister, the country's President now stands alone and unchallenged." *Twitter*, 6 May 2016, twitter.com/NewYorker/status/ 728676985254379520.

Note that the author element is flexible. If you are discussing the work of a film director, for example, the director's name should be placed in the author element, with a descriptor.

> Hitchcock, Alfred, director. *The Lady Vanishes.* United Artists, 1938.

If, on the other hand, you are discussing film editing, you would place the film editor in the author element. In this case, you might also include Hitchcock's name in the "Other Contributors" element.

> Dearing, R.E., film editor. *The Lady Vanishes*, directed by Alfred Hitchcock, United Artists, 1938.

If no single contributor's work is of particular importance in your discussion of a film or television source, omit the author element altogether.

> "The Buys." *The Wire*, created by David Simon and Ed Burns, directed by Peter Medak, season 1, episode 3, HBO, 16 June 2002, disc 1.

If you are citing a **translated source** and the translation itself is the focus of your work, the translator or translators can be placed in the author element.

> Lodge, Kirsten, translator. *Notes from the Underground*. By Fyodor Dostoevsky, edited by Kirsten Lodge, Broadview Press, 2014.

When the work itself is the focus, as is usually the case, the author should remain in the author element, and the translator moved to the "other contributors" element:

> Dostoevsky, Fyodor. *Notes from the Underground*. Translated and edited by Kirsten Lodge, Broadview Press, 2014.

This principle holds true across media and elements. Adapt the MLA structure to create citations that are clear, most relevant to your work, and most useful to your reader.

Title of Source

The title of your source follows the author element. Copy the title as you find it in the source, but with MLA-standard capitalization and punctuation. Capitalize the first word, the last word, and all key words, but not articles, prepositions, coordinating conjunctions, or the *to* in infinitives.

> Carson, Anne. *The Albertine Workout*. New Directions, 2014.

If there is a **subtitle**, include it after the main title, following a colon.

> Bök, Christian. *The Xenotext: Book 1*. Coach House Books, 2015.

Your title gives the reader information about the source. Italicized titles indicate that the source is a complete, independent whole. A title enclosed in quotation marks tells the reader that the source is part of a larger work.

A **book** is an independent whole, so the title is italicized.

> Wordsworth, William. *Poems, in Two Volumes*. Edited by Richard Matlak, Broadview Press, 2016.

Other examples include **long poems** (*In Memoriam*), **magazines** (*The New Yorker*), **newspapers** (*The Guardian*), **journals** (*The American Poetry Review*), **Websites** (*The Camelot Project*), **films** (*Memento*), **television shows** (*The X-Files*), and **compact discs** or **record albums** (*Dark Side of the Moon*).

A **poem**, **short story**, or **essay** within a larger collection is placed in quotation marks.

> Wordsworth, William. "The Solitary Reaper." *Poems, in Two Volumes*, edited by Richard Matlak, Broadview Press, 2016, p. 153.

Other examples include **chapters in books** ("The Autist Artist" in *The Man Who Mistook His Wife for a Hat and Other Clinical Tales*), **encyclopedia articles** ("Existentialism"), **essays in books or journals** ("Salvation in the Garden: Daoism and Ecology" in *Daoism and Ecology: Ways within a Cosmic Landscape*), **short stories** ("Young Goodman Brown"), **short poems** ("Daddy"), **pages on Websites** ("The Fisher King" from *The Camelot Project*), **episodes of television shows** ("Small Potatoes" from *The X-Files*), and **songs** ("Eclipse" from *Dark Side of the Moon*). Put the titles of **public lectures** in double quotation marks as well ("Walls in *The Epic of Gilgamesh*").

These formatting rules apply across media forms. A Website is placed in italics; a posting on the Website is placed in quotation marks.

> Stein, Sadie. "Casting the Runes." *The Daily: The Paris Review Blog*, 9 Oct. 2015, www.theparisreview.org/blog/2015/10/09/casting-the-runes/.

If the title of a stand-alone work contains the title of a work that is not independent, the latter is put in double quotation marks, and the entire title is put in italics (*"Self-Reliance" and Other Essays*). If the title of a stand-alone work appears within the title of another independent work, MLA recommends that the latter be put in italics and the former not (*Chaucer's* House of Fame: *The Poetics of Skeptical Fideism*). If the title of a non-independent work is embedded in another title of the same kind, put the inner title into single quotation marks and the outer title in double quotation marks ("The Drama of Donne's 'The Indifferent'").

When a stand-alone work appears in a **collection**, the work's title remains in italics.

> James, Henry. *The American. Henry James: Novels 1871-1880*, edited by William T. Stafford, Library of America, 1983.

Title of Container

Very often your source is found within a larger context, such as an **anthology**, **periodical**, **newspaper**, **digital platform**, or **Website**. When this is the case, the larger whole is called the "container." For an article in a newspaper, for example, the article is the "source" and the newspaper is the "container." For a song in an **album**, the song is the "source" and the album is the "container."

The title of the container is usually italicized and followed by a comma.

> Gladwell, Malcolm. "The Art of Failure: Why Some People Choke and Others Panic." *The New Yorker*, 21 Aug. 2000, www.newyorker.com/magazine/2000/08/21/the-art-of-failure. Accessed 18 Feb. 2013.

The container can be a Website; a book that is a collection of stories, poems, plays, or essays; a magazine; a journal; an album; or a database.

When doing research, particularly online, one often comes across nested containers, in which, for example, an article is found in a collection of essays, which is itself found on a database. All containers are recorded in the citation, so your reader knows exactly how to find your source. Add more Container elements as needed. Additional containers should follow the period at the end of the information given for the preceding container (usually after the date or location element).

It can be helpful to see this process charted out. Notice that the publication information for the container follows that of the source.

Here is an example of an **article from a periodical**, accessed from an online database.

1. Author.	Sohmer, Steve.
2. Title of source.	"12 June 1599: Opening Day at Shakespeare's Globe."
CONTAINER 1:	
3. Title of container,	*Early Modern Literary Studies: A Journal of Sixteenth- and Seventeenth-Century English Literature,*
4. Other contributors,	
5. Version,	
6. Number,	vol. 3, no.1,
7. Publisher,	

8. Publication Date,	1997.
9. Location.	
CONTAINER 2:	
3. Title of container,	*ProQuest,*
4. Other contributors,	
5. Version,	
6. Number,	
7. Publisher,	
8. Publication Date,	
9. Location.	www.extra.shu.ac.uk/emls/ emlshome.html.

Citation as It Would Appear in Works Cited List:

Sohmer, Steve. "12 June 1599: Opening Day at Shakespeare's Globe." *Early Modern Literary Studies: A Journal of Sixteenth- and Seventeenth-Century English Literature*, vol. 3, no.1, 1997. *ProQuest,* www.extra .shu.ac.uk/emls/emlshome.html.

The next example is an **e-book version** of Jane Austen's *Emma*, accessed from a publisher's Website. The novel is self-contained, so no title of a container is given until the digital platform information is recorded in the second container.

1. **Author.**	Austen, Jane.
2. **Title of source.**	*Emma.*
CONTAINER 1:	
3. **Title of container,**	
4. **Other contributors,**	Edited by Kristen Flieger Samuelian,
5. **Version,**	
6. **Number,**	
7. **Publisher,**	
8. **Publication Date,**	2004.
9. **Location.**	
CONTAINER 2:	
3. **Title of container,**	*Broadview Press,*
4. **Other contributors,**	
5. **Version,**	
6. **Number,**	
7. **Publisher,**	
8. **Publication Date,**	
9. **Location.**	www.broadviewpress.com/ product/emma/#tab-description.

MLA Style

Citation as It Would Appear in Works Cited List:

> Austen, Jane. *Emma*. Edited by Kristen Flieger Samuelian, 2004. *Broadview Press*, www.broadviewpress.com/product/emma/#tab-description. Accessed 5 Feb. 2016.

The elements are recorded sequentially to create your citation. Notice that any elements that don't apply to this source are left out. Any element that is the same for both containers (in this case, the publisher) is recorded in the last (here the second) container; however, the location of this e-book (the Website) contains the name of the publisher, so in this case the publisher field is left empty. This removes the need to repeat information in the citation.

Here is an example citation of a **performance in a television series**, accessed on Netflix.

1. Author.	Spacey, Kevin, performer.
2. Title of source.	"Chapter 5."
CONTAINER 1:	
3. Title of container,	*House of Cards*,
4. Other contributors,	directed by Joel Schumacher,
5. Version,	
6. Number,	season 1, episode 5,
7. Publisher,	
8. Publication Date,	2013.
9. Location.	

CONTAINER 2:	
3. Title of container,	Netflix,
4. Other contributors,	
5. Version,	
6. Number,	
7. Publisher,	
8. Publication Date,	
9. Location.	www.netflix.com/search/house?jbv=70178217&jbp=0&jbr=021.

Citation as It Would Appear in Works Cited List:

Spacey, Kevin, performer. "Chapter 5." *House of Cards*, directed by Joel Schumacher, season 1, episode 5, 2013. *Netflix*, www.netflix.com/search/house?jbv=70178217&jbp=0&jbr=021.

Notice that in this case Netflix produced the show, so the publisher field is left empty in both containers. If the source had been an episode from a series produced by, for example, the BBC, you would include the BBC as publisher.

Tennant, David, performer. "Gridlock." *Dr. Who*, directed by Richard Clark, series 3, episode 3, BBC, 2007. *Netflix*, www.netflix.com/search/dr%20who?jbv=70142441&jbp=0&jbr=0.

Other Contributors

There may be other key people who should be credited in your citation as contributors. This element follows the title of the source and the container (if there is one). The MLA recommends that you include the names of contributors who are important to your research, or if they help your reader to identify the source. Before each name, place a description of the role (do not abbreviate):

adapted by
directed by
edited by
illustrated by
introduction by
narrated by
performance by
translated by

If your listing of a contributor follows the source title, it is capitalized (following a period). If the contributor follows a container, it will be lower-case (following a comma).

Lao Tzu. *Tao Te Ching: A Book about the Way and the Power of the Way.* Translated by Ursula K. Le Guin. Shambhala, 1997.

James, Henry. *The American. Henry James: Novels 1871-1880,* edited by William T. Stafford, Library of America, 1983.

In the Other Contributors element, include the most relevant contributors not already mentioned in the author element. If you are writing about a television episode and a certain performance is one of the elements you discuss, for example, include the performer's name in the Other Contributors element, along with any other contributors you wish to include.

> Medak, Peter, director. "The Buys." *The Wire*, created by David Simon and Ed Burns, performance by Dominic West, season 1, episode 3, HBO, 16 June 2002.

Note that the MLA guidelines are flexible; for this part of the citation especially, consider what your readers most need to know about your source and include that information. Note also that there is some flexibility in the author element; if a particular performance or other contribution is the major focus in your discussion of source, it can be cited in the author element instead.

Version

If your source is **one of several editions**, or if it is a **revised version**, record those details in this element of your citation, followed by a comma. The word "edition" is abbreviated in your citation (ed.).

> Fowles, John. *The Magus*. Rev. ed., Jonathan Cape, 1977.

> Shelley, Mary. *Frankenstein*. Edited by D.L. Macdonald and Kathleen Sherf, 3rd ed., Broadview Press, 2012.

You may also come across **expanded editions**, **revised editions**, and **updated editions**, all of which can be noted in this element of your citation. Different media might use different terminology. For example in film you may find a

director's cut, or in music an **abridged version** of a concerto: use the same principles as above, providing the relevant information in the Version element of your citation.

> Coen, Ethan and Joel Coen, directors. *Blood Simple.* Director's cut, Universal, 2001.

Number

If your source is part of a **multi-volumed work**, or if it is part of a journal that is issued in numbers and/or volumes, include the volume information in this Number element of your citation.

If you are citing **two or more volumes** of a multi-volume work, the entry should note the total number of volumes. If you cite only one of the volumes, list it after the title.

> Jeeves, Julie, editor. *A Reference Guide to Spanish Architecture.* 3 vols, Hackett, 2005.

> Mercer, Bobby, editor. *A Reference Guide to French Architecture.* Vol. 1, Hackett, 2002.

Include the **volume and issue numbers** for journals. Use the abbreviations *vol.* for volume and *no.* for issue number.

> Gregory, Elizabeth. "Marianne Moore's 'Blue Bug': A Dialogic Ode on Celebrity, Race, Gender, and Age." *Modernism/Modernity*, vol. 22, no. 4, 2015, pp. 759–86.

Some journals do not use volume numbers and give only an issue number.

> Sanger, Richard. "Goodbye, Seamus." *Brick*, no. 93, Summer 2014, pp. 153–57.

The Number element is also where you record issue numbers for comic books, or the season and episode numbers for a television series.

> Spacey, Kevin, performer. "Chapter 5." *House of Cards*,
> directed by Joel Schumacher, season 1, episode 5,
> 2013. *Netflix*, www.netflix.com/search/ house?jbv=
> 70178217&jbp=0&jbr=021.

Publisher

In this element of your citation, record the organization that produced the source, whether it be publisher of a book, the organization running a Website, or the studio producing a film. (In the case of a secondary container, include the organization that produced the container.) Do not abbreviate, except in the case of university presses, which may be abbreviated as *UP*.

To find the publisher of a **book**, look on the title page or on the copyright page.

> Dickens, Charles. *The Uncommercial Traveller*. Edited
> by Daniel Tyler, Oxford UP, 2015.

> Rush, Rebecca. *Kelroy*. Edited by Betsy Klimasmith,
> Broadview Press, 2016.

For a **film** or **television series**, the studio or company that produced the show is recorded in the information on the back of a DVD or in the opening and closing credits.

> Simon, David, creator. *The Wire*. HBO, 2002–2008.

For **Websites**, the publisher's information can often be found in the copyright notice at the bottom of the page.

MLA Style

Bogan, Louise. "Women." 1922. *Representative Poetry Online*, edited by Ian Lancashire, University of Toronto, 2000.

A **blog network** may be cited as the publisher of the blogs it hosts.

Cairney, Paul, and Kathryn Oliver. "If scientists want to influence policymaking, they need to understand it." *Political Science*, The Guardian Science Blog Network, 27 Apr. 2016.

You may omit a publisher's name in the following kinds of publications:

- A periodical (journal, magazine, newspaper).
- A work published by its author or editor.
- A Website whose title is essentially the same as the name of the publisher.
- A Website not involved in producing the works it is making available (YouTube, JSTOR, ProQuest). These are listed as containers, but not as publishers.

If **two or more publishers** are listed for your source, cite them both and separate them with a forward slash (/).

Banting, Keith G., editor. *Thinking Outside the Box: Innovation in Policy Ideas.* School of Policy Studies, Queen's University / McGill–Queen's University Press, 2015.

Publication Date

In this element of your citation, record the date of publication for your source. For **books**, this date is found on the copyright page (and sometimes on the title page). If several editions are listed, use the date for the edition you have consulted.

> Stevenson, Robert Louis. *Strange Case of Dr. Jekyll and Mr. Hyde*. Edited by Martin A. Danahay, 3rd ed., Broadview Press, 2015.

Online sources almost always have a date posted, and this is the date you should record in this element.

> Heller, Nathan. "The Big Uneasy: What's Roiling the Liberal-Arts Campus?" *The New Yorker*, 30 May 2016, www.newyorker.com/magazine/2016 /05/30/the-new-activism-of-liberal-arts-colleges.

A source may be associated with **more than one publication date**. An article online may have been previously published in print, or an article printed in a book may have been published previously in a periodical. In this case, the MLA recommends that you record the date that is most relevant to your use of the source. If you consulted the online version of an article, for example, ignore the date of print publication and cite the online publication date.

For books, we record the year of publication. For other sources, whether to include a year, month, and day depends on your source and the context in which you are using it. If you are citing an **episode from a television series**, for example, it is usually enough to record the year it aired.

> Medak, Peter, director. "The Buys." *The Wire*, created by David Simon and Ed Burns, season 1, episode 3, HBO, 2002.

If, however, the context surrounding the episode is being discussed in your work, you should be more specific about the date:

> Medak, Peter, director. "The Buys." *The Wire*, created by David Simon and Ed Burns, season 1, episode 3, HBO, 16 June 2002.

For a **video posted on a Website**, include the date on which the video was posted. In the example below, the posting date should be included in the second container, which records the details for the digital platform. The date the video was released is included in the publication details for the source.

> Gleeson, Thomas, director. *Home*. Screen Innovation Production, 2012. *Vimeo*, uploaded by Thomas Gleeson, 31 Jan. 2013, www.vimeo.com/58630796.

If you are citing a **comment posted on a Web page**, and the time the content was posted is indicated, include the time in your entry.

> Evan. Comment on "Another Impasse on Gun Bills, Another Win for Hyperpolitics." *The New York Times*, 21 June 2016, 9:02 a.m., www.nytimes.com/2016/06/22/us/politics/washington-congress-gun-control.html.

Larger projects are created over a longer span of time. If you are documenting a Web project as a whole, include the full range of years during which it was developed.

> Secord, James A. et al., editors. *Darwin Correspondence Project*. 1974–2016, www.darwinproject.ac.uk/.

The dates of publication for **periodicals** vary. Include in full the information provided by the copyright page, whether it be indicated by season, year, month, week, or day.

> Sanger, Richard. "Goodbye, Seamus." *Brick*, no. 93, Summer 2014, pp. 153–57.

> Trousdale, Rachel. "'Humor Saves Steps': Laughter and Humanity in Marianne Moore." *Journal of Modern Literature,* vol. 35, no. 3, 2012, pp.121–38. *JSTOR,* www.jstor.org/stable/10.2979/jmodelite.35.3.121.

Location

The content of the Location element varies considerably between print, digital, and other sources.

For **print sources** within a periodical or anthology, record a page number (preceded by p.) or a range of page numbers (preceded by pp.).

> Gregory, Elizabeth. "Marianne Moore's 'Blue Bug': A Dialogic Ode on Celebrity, Race, Gender, and Age." *Modernism/Modernity*, vol. 22, no. 4, 2015, pp. 759–86.

> Walcott, Derek. "The Sea Is History." *The Broadview Anthology of Poetry*, edited by Herbert Rosengarten and Amanda Goldrick Jones, Broadview Press, 1992, p. 757.

> Wills, Garry. "A Masterpiece on the Rise of Christianity." Review of *Through the Eye of a Needle: Wealth, The Fall of Rome, and the Making of Christianity in the West, 350–550 AD*, by Peter Brown. *New York Review of Books,* 11 Oct. 2012, pp. 43–45.

An **online work** is located by its URL, or Web address. When copying the URL into your citation, remove the *http://*; this means that usually the URL will begin with *www*. If you need to break a URL over two or more lines, do not insert any hyphens at the break point; instead, when possible, break after a colon or slash or before other marks of punctuation.

> Trousdale, Rachel. "'Humor Saves Steps': Laughter and Humanity in Marianne Moore." *Journal of Modern Literature* vol. 35, no. 3, 2012, pp. 121–38. *JSTOR,* www.jstor.org/stable/10.2979/jmodelite.35.3.121.

Some publishers assign DOIs (Digital Object Identifiers) to their online publications, and these, when available, are preferable to URLs, as they do not change when the source moves (whereas URLs do). If your source has no DOI but offers a "stable" URL, choose that one to include in your citation. The publisher in this case has agreed not to change the URL.

> Yearling, R. "*Hamlet* and the Limits of Narrative." *Essays in Criticism: A Quarterly Journal of Literary Criticism,* vol. 65, no. 4, 2015, pp. 368–82. *Proquest,* doi:dx.doi.org/10.1093/escrit/cgv022.

We find a **television episode** on a DVD by its disc number. Place the disc number in the Location element.

> "The Buys." *The Wire,* created by David Simon and Ed Burns, directed by Peter Medak, season 1, episode 3, HBO, 2002, disc 1.

For a **work of art** that you have seen in person, cite the name of the institution and city where you saw it in the Location element. Leave out the name of the city if the city name is part of the institution name (e.g. The Art Institute of Chicago).

> Sargent, John Singer. *Henry James*. 1913, National Portrait Gallery, London.

Some **archived sources** have a different system for locating objects in the archive. Where this is the case, include the code or number in the Location element.

> Blake, William. *The Marriage of Heaven and Hell*. 1790–1793. The Fitzwilliam Museum, Cambridge, 123-1950. Illuminated printed book.

If you are citing a **live performance** or **lecture**, name the location and the city. Omit the city name if it is part of the location name.

> Royal Winnipeg Ballet. *The Princess and the Goblin*. Directed and choreographed by Twyla Tharp, performances by Paloma Herrera and Dmitri Dovgoselets, 17 Oct. 2012, Centennial Concert Hall, Winnipeg.

Optional Elements

You may include any of the following elements in your citation if you think they are helpful to your reader.

Date of Original Publication
If your source has been republished, it may give your reader some important context if you include the date

MLA Style

of original publication. If you do so, place the date immediately after the source title and close with a period.

> Trollope, Anthony. *The Eustace Diamonds*. 1873. Edited by Stephen Gill and John Sutherland, Penguin, 1986.

City of Publication

Including the city of publication is not very useful these days, so the MLA has decided to remove this element from citations. There are two situations, however, where you may wish to include the city. If the book was published before 1900, the city of publication is associated more closely with the source than the publisher. For these books, you may substitute the city of publication for the publisher.

> Dickens, Charles. *Our Mutual Friend*. Vol. 1, New York, 1800.

Some publishers release more than one version of a text in different countries (a British and an American edition, for example). In you are reading an unexpected version of a text, or the version you are reading has historical significance, place the name of the city in front of the publisher.

> Lawrence, D.H. *Lady Chatterley's Lover*. London, Penguin, 1960.

Books in a Series

If your source is a book in a series, you may add the series name in roman (i.e., without italics) at the end of your citation, preceded by a period.

> Shakespeare, William. *As You Like It*. Edited by David Bevington, Broadview Press, 2012. Broadview Internet Shakespeare Editions.

Unexpected Type of Work

If your source needs further explanation, place a descriptive term (e-mail, transcript, broadcast, street performance, talk, address) at the end of the citation, preceded by a period.

> Rosenheim, Jeff. "Diane Arbus." Art Gallery of Ontario,
> 6 May 2016, Toronto. Lecture.

Date of Access

It is optional to include a date of access for your online citations, but it can be a good idea, particularly if the source does not have a date of publication.

> Crawford, Isabella Valancy. "The Canoe." *Representative Poetry Online*, edited by Ian Lancashire, Web Development Group, Information Technology Services, University of Toronto Libraries, www.tspace.library.utoronto.ca/html/1807/4350/poem596.html. Accessed November 24 2015.

MLA Style

Examples

The following are examples of MLA-style citations for sources across various media. While these examples can offer useful guidance, remember that the MLA guidelines may be adapted to suit the details of the sources you are documenting, as well as the context in which you are using them.

21. single author:

> Graham, Jorie. *From the New World*. Ecco, 2015.
> Malory, Thomas. *Le Morte D'Arthur: Selections*. Edited by Maureen Okun, Broadview Press, 2014.

22. two authors:

> Auden, W.H. and Louis MacNiece. *Letters from Iceland.* Faber & Faber, 2002.
>
> Rectenwald, Michael, and Lisa Carl. *Academic Writing, Real World Topics.* Broadview Press, 2015.

23. three or more authors:

> Blais, Andre, et al. *Anatomy of a Liberal Victory.* Broadview Press, 2002.
>
> Fromkin, Victoria, et al. *An Introduction to Language.* 4th Canadian ed., Nelson, 2010.

24. corporate author:

> *2014 Annual Report.* Broadview Press, 2015.
>
> "History of the Arms and Great Seal of the Commonwealth of Massachusetts." Commonwealth of Massachusetts, www.sec.state.ma.us/pre/presea/sealhis/htm. Accessed 9 May 2016.
>
> Ontario, Ministry of Natural Resources. *Achieving Balance: Ontario's Long-Term Energy Plan.* Queen's Printer for Ontario, 2016, www.energy.gov.on.ca/en/ltep/achieving-balance-ontarios-long-term-energy-plan. Accessed 10 May 2016.

25. works with an anonymous author: Works with an anonymous author should be alphabetized by title.

> *Beowulf.* Edited and translated by R. M. Liuzza. 2nd ed., Broadview Press, 2012.

26. two or more works by the same author: The author's name should appear for the first entry only; for subsequent entries substitute three hyphens for the name of the author.

Menand, Louis. "Bad Comma: Lynne Truss's Strange Grammar." Review of *Eats, Shoots and Leaves*, by Lynne Truss. *The New Yorker*, 28 June 2004, www.newyorker.com/magazine/2004/06/28/bad-comma. Accessed 18 Feb. 2013.

---. *The Metaphysical Club: A Story of Ideas in America*. Farrar, Straus and Giroux, 2001.

27. works under a pseudonym: These are given using the same formatting as author's names. Online usernames are given as they appear.

@newyorker. "With the resignation of Turkey's Prime Minister, the country's President now stands alone and unchallenged." *Twitter*, 6 May 2016, twitter.com/NewYorker/status/ 728676985254379520.

28. edited works:

Renker, Elizabeth, editor. *Poems: A Concise Anthology*. Broadview Press, 2016.

When referring to an edited version of a work written by another author or authors, list the editor(s) after the title.

Trollope, Anthony. *The Eustace Diamonds*. 1873. Edited by Stephen Gill and John Sutherland, Penguin, 1986.

29. works in translation:
The translator is normally listed in the Other Contributors element of the citation.

Bolaño, Roberto. *By Night in Chile*. Translated by Chris Andrews, New Directions, 2003.

MLA Style

If your work focuses on the translation itself, you may list the translator in the author element, moving the author to the Other Contributors element.

> Andrews, Chris, translator. *By Night in Chile*. By
> Roberto Bolaño, New Directions, 2003.

30. selections from anthologies or collections of readings: A selection from a collection of readings or an anthology should begin with the name of the author of the selection. If they are available, be sure to add the selection's inclusive page numbers after the anthology's publication date.

> Crawford, Isabella Valancy. "The Canoe." *Representative
> Poetry Online*, edited by Ian Lancashire, U of
> Toronto, 1997, www.rpo.library.utoronto.ca/
> poems/canoe. Accessed 20 Apr. 2015.
>
> Gleach, Frederic W. "Controlled Speculation: Inter-
> preting the Saga of Pocahontas and Captain John
> Smith." *Reading Beyond Words: Contexts for Native
> History*, edited by Jennifer S. H. Brown and Eliza-
> beth Vibert, Broadview Press, 1996, pp. 21–42.
>
> Mahfouz, Naguib. "Half a Day." *The Picador Book of
> African Stories*, edited by Stephen Gray, Picador,
> 2001, pp. 3–6.

31. cross-references for works from the same collection or anthology: It can be more efficient to create a full entry for the collection or anthology, and then to list each cited item in its own entry. Position the entries in the Works Cited list alphabetically, as you normally would, and use a short form for the collection or anthology, as in the following example:

Brown, Jennifer S. H., and Elizabeth Vibert, editors. *Reading Beyond Words: Contexts for Native History.* Broadview Press, 1996.

Cruikshank, Julie. "Discovery of Gold on the Klondike: Perspectives from Oral Tradition." Brown and Vibert, pp. 433–59.

Gleach, Frederic W. "Controlled Speculation: Interpreting the Saga of Pocahontas and Captain John Smith." Brown and Vibert, pp. 21–42.

32. multi-volume works: If you are citing one or more of the volumes, list them after the title. The entry may note the total number of volumes at the end of the citation (this is optional).

Mercer, Bobby, editor. *A Reference Guide to French Architecture.* Vol. 1, Hackett, 2002. 3 vols.

Jeeves, Julie, editor. *A Reference Guide to Spanish Architecture.* 3 vols., Hackett, 2005.

33. different editions: The edition should be specified whenever it is not the first edition. Include whatever the title page indicates about the particular edition, and use abbreviations (e.g., *rev. ed.* for *revised edition, 2nd ed.* for *second edition,* and so on).

Fowles, John. *The Magus.* Rev. ed. by Jonathan Cape, 1977.

Shelley, Mary. *Frankenstein.* 1818. Edited by Lorne Macdonald and Kathleen Scherf, 2nd ed., Broadview Press, 1999.

The Bible. Authorized King James Version, Oxford UP, 2008.

MLA Style

34. republished sources: When a source was previously published in a different form, you may include information about the prior publication. This is an optional element; include this information at your discretion, if you feel it would give your reader important context for the source.

> MacMillan, Margaret. "Hubris." *History's People: Personalities and the Past*, Massey Lectures, CBC Radio, 3 Nov. 2015, www.cbc.ca/radio/ideas/history-s-people-personalities-the-past-lecture-2-1.3301571. Podcast. Originally delivered at the Arts and Culture Centre, St. John's, NL, 25 Sept. 2015, 7:00 p.m. Lecture.

35. reference work entries: List by the author of the entry, if known; otherwise, list by the entry itself. The citation of a well-known reference work (because such works are frequently updated) should not have full publication details; provide the edition number, date, and location only. Don't include page numbers for works that arrange their entries alphabetically.

> "Artificial." *Oxford English Dictionary.* 2nd ed., 1989.
> Fowler, H.W. "Unique." *The King's English*, 2nd ed., 1908. *Bartleby.com*, bartleby.com/116/108.html#2. Accessed 5 Mar. 2016.
> Marsh, James. "Canoe, Birchbark." *The Canadian Encyclopedia*, 2000 ed., McClelland & Stewart, 1999.

36. works with a title in the title: A title that is usually italicized should remain italicized when it appears within quotation marks:

Yearling, R. "*Hamlet* and the Limits of Narrative." *Essays in Criticism: A Quarterly Journal of Literary Criticism,* vol. 65, no. 4, 2015, pp. 368–82. *Proquest,* doi:dx.doi.org/10.1093/escrit/cgv022

Titles that are in quotation marks that appear within other titles in quotation marks are enclosed by single quotation marks:

Bettelheim, Bruno. "'The Goose Girl': Achieving Autonomy." *The Uses of Enchantment: The Meaning and Importance of Fairy Tales,* Vintage-Random House, 1989, pp. 136–43.

An italicized title that is included within another italicized title is neither italicized nor placed in quotation marks. It appears in roman:

Morelli, Stefan. *Stoppard's* Arcadia *and Modern Drama.* Ashgate, 2004.

If a title normally enclosed in quotation marks appears in an italicized title, keep the quotation marks:

Wimsatt, C.W. *"Fern Hill" and British Poetry in the 1950s.* ECW, 2004.

37. material from prefaces, introductions, etc.: If you refer to something from a work's preface, introduction, or foreword, the reference under Works Cited should begin with the name of the author of that preface, introduction, or foreword. Add inclusive page numbers after the date of publication.

Warkentin, Germaine. Introduction. *Set in Authority,* by Sara Jeannette Duncan, Broadview Press, 1996, pp. 9–51.

38. magazine articles: The title of the article should appear in quotation marks, the title of the magazine in italics. If no author is identified, the title of the article should appear first. If the magazine is published monthly or every two months, give the date as month and year. For magazines published weekly or every two weeks, give the date as day, month, and year. Abbreviate the names of months (except for *May*, *June*, and *July*).

> MacRitchie, Lynn. "Ofili's Glittering Icons." *Art in America,* Jan. 2000, pp. 44–56.

> "Greens in Pinstriped Suits." *The Economist.* 21 May 2016, www.economist.com/news/business/21699141-climate-conscious-shareholders-are-putting-big-oil-spot-greens-pinstriped-suits.

If you accessed the article online yourself, you may include the date of access, though it is an optional element. If the Website is hosted by a body other than the magazine itself, include it as a second container with its accompanying publication details.

> Gladwell, Malcolm. "The Art of Failure: Why Some People Choke and Others Panic." *The New Yorker,* 21 Aug. 2000, www.newyorker.com/magazine/2000/08/21/the-art-of-failure. Accessed 18 Feb. 2013.

> Kreimer, Julian. "Mernet Larsen." *Art in America*, vol. 104, no. 4, 2016, pp. 115–116. *Academic Search Complete*, www.search.ebscohost.com/login.aspx?direct=true&db=a9hAN=114088897&site=ehost-live. Accessed 4 Nov. 2015.

39. newspaper articles: The basic principles to follow with newspaper articles or editorials are the same as with magazine articles (see above). Note, however, that when the newspaper's sections are paginated separately, section as well as page numbers are often required. If an article is not printed on consecutive pages, include only the first page number followed by a plus sign. In the following reference the article begins on page 3 of the first section:

> Yakabuski, Konrad. "Many Looking for Meaning in Vice-Presidential Debate." *The Globe and Mail,* 12 Oct. 2012, p. A3+.

If you are citing an online version of a newspaper article you should include the date you accessed the site. The site name, if it is different from the container title, should also be included.

> Kaplan, Thomas. "Bernie Sanders Wins Oregon; Hillary Clinton Declares Victory in Kentucky." *The New York Times,* 17 May 2016, www.nytimes.com/2016/05/18/us/politics/bernie-sanders-oregon-results.html. Accessed 17 May 2016.

40. journal articles: The basic principles are the same as with magazine articles, but entries for journal articles include the volume and issue numbers.

> Roy, Indrani. "Irony and Derision in Congreve's *The Way of the World.*" *PMLA,* vol. 120, no.6, 2005, pp. 60–72.

If you are citing an online version of a journal article you should include the date you accessed the site, as well as any additional containers and their publication details (databases, for example).

Sohmer, Steve. "12 June 1599: Opening Day at Shakespeare's Globe." *Early Modern Literary Studies: A Journal of Sixteenth- and Seventeenth-Century English Literature*, vol. 3, no.1, 1997. *ProQuest,* www.extra.shu.ac.uk/emls/emlshome.html. Accessed 18 May 2016.

41. book reviews: The name of the reviewer (if it has been provided) should come first, followed by the title of the review (if there is one), and the information on the book itself.

Leiter, Brian, and Michael Weisberg. "Do You Only Have a Brain? On Thomas Nagel." Review of *Why the Materialist Neo-Darwinian Conception of Nature Is Almost Certainly False*, by Thomas Nagel, *The Nation,* 22 Oct. 2012, www.thenation.com/article/do-you-only-have-brain-thomas-nagel/. Accessed 22 Oct. 2012.

Wills, Garry. "A Masterpiece on the Rise of Christianity." Review of *Through the Eye of a Needle: Wealth, The Fall of Rome, and the Making of Christianity in the West, 350–550 AD*, by Peter Brown, *New York Review of Books,* 11 Oct. 2012, pp. 43–45.

42. periodical publications in online databases:

Hill, Katherine C. "Virginia Woolf and Leslie Stephen: History and Literary Revolution." *PMLA*, vol. 96, no.3, 1981, pp. 351–62. *JSTOR*, www.jstor.org/stable/461911. Accessed 6 Oct. 2012.

43. illustrated books: Include the illustrator's name as well as the author's name.

Juster, Norman. *The Phantom Tollbooth*. Illustrated by
Jules Feiffer, Yearling-Random House, 1961.

44. graphic narratives: In many graphic narratives, both the
illustrations and the text are created by one person; these
kinds of works should be documented as in the first example
below. Use the second example's format for works whose
text is by one person and illustrations by another.

Leavitt, Sarah. *Tangles: A Story about Alzheimer's, My
Mother, and Me*. Freehand Books, 2010.

Pekar, Harvey. *Ego and Hubris: The Michael Malice
Story*. Art by Gary Dumm, Ballantine-Random
House, 2006.

45. films or television episodes: These entries may be tai-
lored to the context in which you are citing the work. If you
are discussing the work of a director, for example, place the
director's name in the Author element:

Zeitlin, Behn, director. *Beasts of the Southern Wild*.
Performances by Quvenzhané Wallis and Dwight
Henry, Fox Searchlight, 2012.

Medak, Peter, director. "The Buys." *The Wire*, created by
David Simon and Ed Burns, season 1, episode 3,
HBO, 16 June 2002.

If you are discussing a particular performance, place the
actor's name in the Author element.

Moss, Elizabeth, performer. "A Little Kiss." *Mad Men*,
directed by Jennifer Getzinger, AMC, 25 Mar. 2012.

Spacey, Kevin, performer. "Chapter 5." *House of Cards*,
directed by Joel Schumacher, season 1, episode
5. *Netflix*, www.netflix.com/search/house?jbv=
70178217&jbp=0&jbr=021.

46. online videos: If your source is a video on a Website, cite, if you can, who uploaded the video, and the date on which the video was posted.

> Gleeson, Thomas, director. "Home." Screen Innovation Production Fund, 2012. *Vimeo*, uploaded by Thomas Gleeson, 31 Jan. 2013, www.vimeo.com/58630796.

47. radio broadcasts:

> "Glenn Gould Special." *The Sunday Edition*, narrated by Robert Harris and Michael Enright, CBC Radio One, 23 Sept. 2012.

48. podcasts:

> "Too Old to Be Governable Too Young to Die Edition." *Slate's Culture Gabfest*, narrated by Stephen Metcalf, Julia Turner, and Laura Miller, 18 May 2016, www.slate.com/articles/podcasts/culturegabfest/2016/05/. Accessed 18 May 2016.

49. recorded music:

> Williams, Lucinda. "Real Love." *Little Honey*, Lost Highway, 2008.

50. live performances: If you are citing a live performance or lecture, include the physical location and the city where the performance or lecture was delivered, as well as the date. Omit the city name if it is part of the location name. Include other information about the performance—the names of the director, the conductor, and/or lead performers, for instance—where such information is relevant. If your work focuses on the contribution of a performance's director, for example, cite that person in the Author element.

Other important contributors follow the title in the Other Contributors element.

> Bedford, Brian, director. *The Importance of Being Earnest*, by Oscar Wilde. Performances by Brian Bedford, Santino Fontana, David Furr, Charlotte Parry, and Sarah Topham, Roundabout Theatre Company, American Airlines Theatre, New York. 3 July 2011.

> MacMillan, Margaret. "Hubris." *History's People: Personalities and the Past*, Arts and Culture Centre, St. John's NL, 25 Sept. 2015, 7:00 p.m. Massey Lecture.

51. works of visual art: When citing a physical object you have experienced, such as a work of art, provide in the Location element the name of the institution and city where you experienced it. Leave out the name of the city if the city name is part of the institution name (e.g. Art Institute of Chicago).

> Housser, Yvonne McKague. *Cobalt.* 1931. National Gallery of Canada, Ottawa.

> Sargent, John Singer. *Henry James.* 1913. National Portrait Gallery, London.

If you access a work of art online or in a book, you should include full information about the Website or volume you consulted.

> Colquhoun, Ithell. *Scylla.* 1938. Tate Gallery, London. *Tate Women Artists*, by Alicia Foster, Tate, 2004, p. 85.

> Giotto di Bondone. *Lamentation.* 1304–06. Capella Scrovegni, Padua, *Web Gallery of Art*, www.wga.hu/frames-e.html?/html/g/giotto/. Accessed 29 Jan. 2013.

MLA Style

52. interviews: Begin all entries for interviews with the name of the person being interviewed, and if there is a title for the interview, include it (in quotation marks if it is part of another work, or in italics if it has been published by itself). If there is no title, or if the title does not make clear that the work is an interview, write *Interview*, and give the name of the interviewer, if known. Finish with whatever publication information is appropriate. If you conducted the interview yourself, give the name of the person you interviewed, the medium (*Personal interview, Telephone interview*), and the date.

> Erdrich, Louise. Interview by Bill Moyers, *Bill Moyers Journal*, PBS, 9 Apr. 2010, www.pbs.org/moyers/journal/04092010/watch2.html. Accessed 16 Jan. 2013.
>
> Nelson, Willie. "The Silver-Headed Stranger." Interview by Andrew Goldman, *New York Times Magazine*, 16 Dec. 2012, p. 12.
>
> Rosengarten, Herbert. Personal interview, 21 Jan. 2013.

53. online projects: In the case of large projects, cite the full range of years during which the project has been developed:

> Secord, James A. et al., editors. *Darwin Correspondence Project*. 1974–2016, www.darwinproject.ac.uk/.
>
> Willett, Perry, editor. *Victorian Women Writers Project*. Indiana University Digital Library Program, 1995–2016, webapp1.dlib.indiana.edu/vwwp/welcome.do. Accessed 26 Nov. 2012.

54. e-books: E-books should be documented according to the same principles as other digital media. Make sure to add a Container element citing the digital platform from which the e-book has been accessed or downloaded.

> Austen, Jane. *Pride and Prejudice*. 1813. *Project Gutenberg*, 2008, www.gutenberg.org/files/1342/1342-h /1342-h.htm. Accessed 20 Feb. 2016.
>
> Emerson, Ralph Waldo. *The American Scholar*. 1837. *American Transcendentalism Web*, ed. Ann Woodlief, Virginia Commonwealth U, 1999, www. transcendentalism-legacy.tamu.edu/authors/ emerson/essays/amscholar.html. Accessed 16 Mar. 2013.
>
> Herman, Jonathan R. *I and Tao: Martin Buber's Encounter with Chuang Tzu*. State U of New York P, 1996. *Google Books*, books.google.ca/ books?id=l1U10Ei8oboC. Downloaded 30 May 2015.
>
> Shakespeare, William. *As You Like It*. Edited by David Bevington, Broadview Press, 2012. *Broadview Press*, www.broadviewpress.com/product/as-you-like-it/#tab-description. Downloaded 3 Mar. 2016.

55. information databases:

> Gaston, Craig. "Consumption-related greenhouse gas emissions in Canada, the United States and China." *Statistics Canada*, 8 Dec. 2011, www.statcan.gc.ca/ pub/16-002-x/2011004/part-partie4-eng.htm. Accessed 17 Apr. 2016.

56. entry in a wiki: Wikis are online sites that can be added to and edited by any site user; as such, they may be subject to frequent changes made by any number of authors and editors. Do not, therefore, provide any authors' names. Start with the entry's title; then give the name of the wiki, the site publisher, the date of the entry's last update, the medium, and the date you accessed the site.

> "William Caxton." *Wikipedia*. Wikimedia Foundation, 20 Oct. 2012, www.en.wikipedia.org/wiki/ William_Caxton. Accessed 26 Oct. 2012.

57. blog post: Include the title of the posting as your source title, the blog title as the first container, and the name of the blog host as a publisher.

> LePan, Don. "Reading and Writing and Work." *Animals, Rising Stories, Etc.*, Blogspot, 21 May 2016, www.donlepan.blogspot.ca. Accessed 24 May 2016.

58. e-mail message: Use the subject as the title and place it within quotation marks.

> Milton, Frank. "Thoughts on Animal Rights." Received by the author, 15 Jan. 2013.

If it is not clear from the context of your work that the source being cited is an e-mail, you may wish to add an optional element to the end of your citation that indicates the type of work.

> Stuart, Jennifer. "My Experience of the Attack." Received by the author, 17 May 2016. E-mail.

59. tweet: Copy the full, unchanged text of the tweet in the title element and enclose it in quotation marks. The username is included as the Author element.

> @newyorker. "With the resignation of Turkey's Prime Minister, the country's President now stands alone and unchallenged." *Twitter*, 6 May 2016, twitter.com/ NewYorker/status/728676985254379520.

60. comment posted on a web page:
Usernames are given in full, unchanged. If the comment is anonymous, skip the author element. If the comment does not have its own title, provide instead a description of the comment that includes the title of the work being commented on (e.g. Comment on "Clinton Aims for Decisive Victory"). If it is available, include the exact time of posting in the Publication Date element.

> Evan. Comment on "Another Impasse on Gun Bills, Another Win for Hyperpolitics." *The New York Times*, 21 June 2016, 9:02 a.m., www.nytimes.com/ 2016/06/22/us/politics/washington-congress-gun- control.html.

O *MLA Style Sample*

Following is a sample excerpt written in MLA style. A complete essay in MLA style may be found at the back of this book. Further sample essays may also be found on the Website associated with this book.

Urban renewal is as much a matter of psychology as it is of bricks and mortar. As Paul Goldberger has described, there have been many plans to revitalize Havana (50–61). But both that city and the community of Cuban exiles in Florida remain haunted by a sense of absence and separation. As Lourdes Casal reminds us, "Exile / is living where there is no house whatever / in which we were ever children" (lines 1–3).

The psychology of outsiders also makes a difference. Part of the reason Americans have not much noticed the dire plight of Miami, their fifth-largest city, is that it does not stir the national imagination (Rybczynski 12). Conversely, there has been far more concern over the state of cities such as New Orleans and Quebec, whose history and architecture excite the romantic imagination. As Nora Phelps has discussed, the past is in itself a key trigger for romantic notions, and cities whose history is particularly visible will engender passionate attachments (par. 3). And as Stephanie Wright and Carole King have detailed, almost all French-speaking Quebecers feel their heritage to be bound up with that of Quebec City (2: 171–74). (Richard Ford's character Frank Bascombe has suggested that "New Orleans defeats itself" by longing for "a mystery it doesn't have and never will, if it ever did" [48; ch. 3] but this remains a minority view.) Georgiana Gibson is also among those who have investigated the interplay between urban psychology and urban reality (*Cities* 64–89). Gibson's personal website now includes a working model she is developing in an attempt to represent the effects of various psychological schemata on the landscape.

The above references connect to Works Cited as follows:

Works Cited

Casal, Lourdes. "Definition." Translated by Elizabeth Macklin, *The New Yorker*, 26 Jan. 1998, p. 79.

Ford, Richard. *The Sportswriter*. 1986. 2nd ed., Vintage-Random House, 1995.

Gibson, Georgiana. *Cities in the Twentieth Century*. Beacon Press, 2011.

---. "Homepage." *Department of Geography*, Brigham Young University, 10 July 2011, www.geography.byu.edu/Pages/Home.aspx.

Goldberger, Paul. "Annals of Preservation: Bringing Back Havana." *The New Republic*, 26 Jan. 2005, pp. 50–62.

Phelps, Nora. "Pastness and the Foundations of Romanticism." *Romanticism and Victorianism on the Net*, vol. 11, no. 3, 2007, www.ravonjournal.org. Accessed 6 July 2013.

Rybczynski, Witold. "The Fifth City." Review of *A Prayer for the City*, by Buzz Bissinger, *The New York Review of Books*, 5 Feb. 1998, pp. 12–14.

Wright, Stephanie, and Carole King. *Quebec: A History*. 2 vols., McGill-Queen's UP, 2012.

Among the details to notice in this referencing system:

- MLA style focuses on the process of documentation, not the prescriptive following of specific guidelines (though consistent formatting according to MLA principles is still vital to communicate clearly with your reader).

- To create a citation, list the relevant elements in the order prescribed by MLA (see the table on page 45). Any elements that don't apply to a given source are left out (placeholders for unknown information like *n.d.* ("no date") are not required).

- Follow the punctuation guidelines in the table on page 45. Any elements recorded after a period should be capitalized; elements following a comma should be lower-case.

- Your citation should give your reader a map to your exact source. If you are documenting an article found in a periodical, for example, which was itself found on a database, you should include the publication details of both "containers" (periodical and database) as part of your citation. See the "Title of Container" section above for details.

- Terms such as *editor, edited by, translator, translated by*, and *review* are not abbreviated.

- If there are three or more authors or editors, only the first name is given, reversed, followed by *et al.*

- Citations for journals include abbreviations for volume and issue ("vol. 40, no. 3").

- Give the publisher's name in full, but drop business words such as "Company." For University presses, use the abbreviations *U, P*, and *UP*.

- City names are not required as part of the publication details.
- The date of access for an online source is optional.
- Page numbers are preceded by *p.* for a single page reference, or *pp.* for a range of pages.
- Include the URL (with *http:* removed) or the DOI in the location element for digital sources. Do not surround the address with angle brackets and do conclude with a period.
- You do not have to identify the media type of your source, unless it is required for clarity.

APA Style

APA Style

APA Style

◎ APA Style

The American Psychological Association (APA) style is used in many behavioral and social sciences. Like MLA style, APA style calls for parenthetical references in the body of a paper, although the main components in these are author and date rather than author and page number. APA also requires that full bibliographical information about the sources be provided in a list called "References" at the end of the essay.

This section outlines the key features of APA style and includes a brief sample at the end of the discussion. A full sample essay can be found at the end of the book. Additional full sample essays in APA style are available on the Broadview website. Go to <http://sites.broadviewpress.com/writing/>. If you have more detailed questions, consult *Concise Rules of APA Style* (6th edition, 2010). You may also find answers at www.apastyle.org.

O *Incorporating Sources in APA Style*

The following material should be read in conjunction with the introductory discussion of citation, documentation, and plagiarism (see pages 12–15).

There are three main ways of working source material into a paper: summaries, paraphrases, and direct quotations. In order to avoid plagiarism, care must be taken with all three kinds of borrowing, both in the way they are handled and in their referencing. In what follows, a passage from page 102 of a book by Terrence W. Deacon (*The Symbolic*

APA Style

Species: The Co-Evolution of Language and the Brain, published in New York City by Norton in 1997) serves as the source for a sample summary, paraphrase, and quotation. The examples feature the APA style of in-text parenthetical citations, but the requirements for presenting the source material are the same for all academic referencing systems.

original source   Over the last few decades language researchers seem to have reached a consensus that language is an innate ability, and that only a significant contribution from innate knowledge can explain our ability to learn such a complex communication system. Without question, children enter the world predisposed to learn human languages. All normal children, raised in normal social environments, inevitably learn their local language, whereas other species, even when raised and taught in this same environment, do not. This demonstrates that human brains come into the world specially equipped for this function.

○ Summarizing

An honest and competent summary, whether of a passage or an entire book, must not only represent the source accurately but also use original wording and include a citation. It is a common misconception that only quotations need to be acknowledged as borrowings in the body of an essay, but without a citation, even a fairly worded summary or paraphrase is an act of plagiarism. The first example below is faulty on two counts: it borrows wording (underlined) from the source, and it has no parenthetical reference.

needs checking   <u>Researchers</u> agree that language learning is <u>innate, and that only innate knowledge can explain</u> how we are able <u>to learn</u> a <u>system</u> of <u>communication</u> that is so <u>complex.</u> <u>Normal children raised in normal</u> ways will always <u>learn their local language, whereas other species do not, even when taught</u> human language and exposed to the <u>same environment</u>.

The next example avoids the wording of the source passage, and a parenthetical citation notes the author and date (but note that no page number is provided, as APA does not require these in citations of summarized material).

revised   There is now wide agreement among linguists that the ease with which human children acquire their native tongues, under the conditions of a normal childhood, demonstrates an inborn capacity for language that is not shared by any other animals, not even those who are reared in comparable ways and given human language training (Deacon, 1997).

O *Paraphrasing*

Whereas a summary is a shorter version of its original, a paraphrase tends to be about the same length. However, paraphrases, like summaries, must reflect their sources accurately while using original wording, and must include a citation. The original material's page number (or paragraph number for a nonpaginated online source) is not absolutely essential for a paraphrase, but APA suggests it be added as an aid to any reader who would like to refer to the original text. What follows is a paraphrase of the first sentence of the Deacon passage, which despite having a proper citation, falls short by being too close to the wording of the original (underlined).

needs checking   Researchers in language have come to a consensus in the past few decades that the acquisition of language is innate; such contributions from knowledge contribute significantly to our ability to master such a complex system of communication (Deacon, 1997, p. 102).

Simply substituting synonyms for the words and phrases of the source, however, is not enough to avoid plagiarism. Even with its original wording, the next example also fails but for a very different reason: it follows the original's sentence structure, as illustrated in the interpolated copy below it.

needs checking   Recently, linguists appear to have come to an agreement that speaking is an in-born skill, and that nothing but a substantial input from in-born cognition can account for the human capacity to acquire such a complicated means of expression (Deacon, 1997, p. 102).

Recently (*over the last few decades*), linguists (*language researchers*) appear to have come to an agreement (*seem to have reached a consensus*) that speaking is an in-born skill (*that language is an innate ability*), and that nothing but a substantial input (*and that only a significant contribution*) from in-born cognition (*from innate knowledge*) can account for the human capacity (*can explain our ability*) to acquire

> such a complicated means of expression (*to learn such a complex communication system*) (Deacon, 1997, p. 102).

What follows is a good paraphrase of the passage's opening sentence; this paraphrase captures the sense of the original without echoing the details and shape of its language.

revised   Linguists now broadly agree that children are born with the ability to learn language; in fact, the human capacity to acquire such a difficult skill cannot easily be accounted for in any other way (Deacon, 1997, p. 102).

O *Quoting Directly*

Unlike paraphrases and summaries, direct quotations must use the exact wording of the original. Because they involve importing outside words, quotations pose unique challenges. Quote too frequently, and you risk making your readers wonder why they are not reading your sources instead of your paper. Your essay should present something you want to say—informed and supported by properly documented sources, but forming a contribution that is yours alone. To that end, use secondary material to help you build a strong framework for your work, not to replace it. Quote sparingly, therefore; use your sources' exact wording only when it is important or particularly memorable.

To avoid misrepresenting your sources, be sure to quote accurately, and to avoid plagiarism, take care to indicate quotations as quotations, and cite them properly. If you use the author's name in a signal phrase, follow it with the date in parentheses, and be sure the verb of the phrase is in the past tense (*demonstrated*) or present perfect tense (*has demonstrated*). For all direct quotations, you must also include the page number (or paragraph number for a nonpaginated online source) of the original in your citation, as in the following examples.

Below are two problematic quotations. The first does not show which words come directly from the source.

needs checking   Deacon (1997) maintained that children enter the world predisposed to learn human languages (p. 102).

The second quotation fails to identify the source at all.

needs checking   Many linguists have argued that "children enter the world predisposed to learn human languages."

The next example corrects both problems by naming the source and indicating clearly which words come directly from it.

revised   Deacon (1997) maintained that "children enter the world predisposed to learn human languages" (p. 102).

◎ FORMATTING QUOTATIONS

There are two ways to signal an exact borrowing: by enclosing it in double quotation marks and by indenting it as a block of text. Which you should choose depends on the length and genre of the quotation and the style guide you are following.

⊙ Short Quotations

What counts as a short quotation differs among the various reference guides. In MLA style, "short" means up to four lines; in APA, up to forty words; and in Chicago Style, up to one hundred words. All the guides agree, however, that short quotations must be enclosed in double quotation marks, as in the examples below.

Short quotation,   According to Deacon (1997), linguists agree that
full sentence: a human child's capacity to acquire language is inborn: "Without question, children enter the world predisposed to learn human languages" (p. 102).

Short quotation,   According to Deacon (1997), linguists agree that
partial sentence: human "children enter the world predisposed to learn human languages" (p. 102).

⊙ Long Quotations

In APA style, longer quotations of forty words or more should be double-spaced and indented, as a block, about one-half inch from the left margin. Do not include quotation marks; the indentation indicates that the words come exactly from the source. Note that indented quotations are often introduced with a full sentence followed by a colon.

> Deacon (1997) maintained that human beings are born with a unique cognitive capacity:
>
> > Without question, children enter the world predisposed to learn human languages. All normal children, raised in normal social environments,

> inevitably learn their local language, whereas other species, even when raised and taught in this same environment, do not. This demonstrates that human brains come into the world specially equipped for this function. (p. 102)

⊙ Quotations within Quotations

You may sometimes find, within the original passage you wish to quote, words already enclosed in double quotation marks. If your quotation is short, enclose it all in double quotation marks, and use single quotation marks for the embedded quotation.

> Deacon (1997) was firm in maintaining that human language differs from other communication systems in kind rather than degree: "Of no other natural form of communication is it legitimate to say that 'language is a more complicated version of that'" (p. 44).

If your quotation is long, keep the double quotation marks of the original. Note as well that in the example below, the source's use of italics (*simple*) is also faithfully reproduced.

> Deacon (1997) was firm in maintaining that human language differs from other communication systems in kind rather than degree:
>
>> Of no other natural form of communication is it legitimate to say that "language is a more complicated version of that." It is just as misleading to call other species' communication systems *simple* languages as it is to call them languages. In addition to asserting that a Procrustean mapping of

one to the other is possible, the analogy ignores the sophistication and power of animals' non-linguistic communication, whose capabilities may also be without language parallels. (p. 44)

⊙ Adding to or Deleting from a Quotation

While it is important to use the original's exact wording in a quotation, it is allowable to modify a quotation somewhat, as long as the changes are clearly indicated and do not distort the meaning of the original. You may want to add to a quotation in order to clarify what would otherwise be puzzling or ambiguous to someone who does not know its context; put whatever you add in square brackets.

● *Using square brackets to add to a quotation*

Deacon (1997) concluded that children are born "specially equipped for this [language] function" (p. 102).

If you would like to streamline a quotation by omitting anything unnecessary to your point, insert an ellipsis (three spaced dots) to show that you've left material out.

● *Using an ellipsis to delete from a quotation*

When the quotation looks like a complete sentence but is actually part of a longer sentence, you should provide an ellipsis to show that there is more to the original than you are using.

Deacon (1997) concluded that "… children enter the world predisposed to learn human languages" (p. 102).

Note the square brackets example above; if the quotation is clearly a partial sentence, ellipses aren't necessary.

When the omitted material runs over a sentence boundary or constitutes a whole sentence or more, insert a period plus an ellipsis.

> Deacon (1997) claimed that human children are born with a unique ability to acquire their native language: "Without question, children enter the world predisposed to learn human languages.... [H]uman brains come into the world specially equipped for this function" (p. 102).

Be sparing in modifying quotations; it is all right to have one or two altered quotations in a paper, but if you find yourself changing quotations often, or adding to and omitting from one quotation more than once, reconsider quoting at all. A paraphrase or summary is very often a more effective choice.

⊙ Integrating Quotations

Quotations must be worked smoothly and grammatically into your sentences and paragraphs. Always, of course, mark quotations as such, but for the purpose of integrating them into your writing, treat them otherwise as if they were your own words. The boundary between what you say and what your source says should be grammatically seamless.

needs checking   Deacon (1997) pointed out, "whereas other species, even when raised and taught in this same environment, do not" (p. 102).

revised   According to Deacon (1997), while human children brought up under normal conditions acquire the language they are exposed to, "other species, even when raised and taught in this same environment, do not" (p. 102).

O *Avoiding "dumped" quotations*

Integrating quotations well also means providing a context for them. Don't merely drop them into your paper or string them together like beads on a necklace; make sure to introduce them by noting where the material comes from and how it connects to whatever point you are making.

needs checking   For many years, linguists have studied how human children acquire language. "Without question, children enter the world predisposed to learn human language" (Deacon, 1997, p. 102).

revised   Most linguists studying how human children acquire language have come to share the conclusion articulated by Deacon (1997): "Without question, children enter the world predisposed to learn human language" (p. 102).

needs checking   "Without question, children enter the world predisposed to learn human language" (Deacon, 1997, p. 102). "There is ... something special about human brains that enables us to do with ease what no other species can do even minimally without intense effort and remarkably insightful training" (Deacon, 1997, p. 103).

revised   Deacon (1997) based his claim that we "enter the world predisposed to learn human language" on the fact that very young humans

can "do with ease what no other species can
do even minimally without intense effort and
remarkably insightful training" (pp. 102–103).

○ *Signal Phrases*

To leave no doubt in your readers' minds about which parts
of your essay are yours and which come from elsewhere,
identify the sources of your summaries, paraphrases, and
quotations with signal phrases, as in the following examples.

- As Carter and Rosenthal (2011) demonstrated …
- According to Ming, Bartlett, and Koch (2014), …
- In his latest article McGann (2015) advanced the
  view that …
- As Beyerstein (2000) observed, …
- Kendal and Ahmadi (1998) have suggested that …
- Freschi (2004) was not alone in rejecting these claims,
  arguing that …
- Cabral, Chernovsky, and Morgan (2015) empha-
  sized this point in their recent research: … •
  Sayeed (2003) has maintained that …
- In a landmark study, Mtele (1992) concluded that …
- In her later work, however, Hardy (2005) overturned
  previous results, suggesting that …

In order to help establish your paper's credibility, you may
also find it useful at times to include in a signal phrase
information that shows why readers should take the source
seriously, as in the following example:

In this insightful and compassionate work, clinical neu-
rologist Oliver Sacks (1985) described …

APA Style

Here, the signal phrase mentions the author's professional credentials; it also points out the importance of his book, which is appropriate to do in the case of a work as famous as Sacks' *The Man Who Mistook His Wife for a Hat*.

Below is a fuller list of words and expressions that may be useful in the crafting of signal phrases:

according to _____,	endorsed
acknowledged	found
added	granted
admitted	illustrated
advanced	implied
agreed	in the view of _____,
allowed	in the words of _____,
argued	insisted
asserted	intimated
attested	noted
believed	observed
claimed	pointed out
commented	put it
compared	reasoned
concluded	refuted
confirmed	rejected
contended	reported
declared	responded
demonstrated	suggested
denied	took issue with
disputed	thought
emphasized	wrote

O *About In-Text Citations*

1. **in-text citation**: The APA system emphasizes the date of publication, which must appear within an in-text citation. Whenever a quotation is given, the page number, preceded by the abbreviation *p.*, must also be provided:

- Bonnycastle (2007) refers to "the true and lively spirit of opposition" (p. 204) with which Marxist literary criticism invigorates the discipline.

It is common to mention in the body of your text the surnames of authors that you are citing, as is done in the example above. If author names are not mentioned in the body of the text, however, they must be provided within the in-text citation. In the example below, note the comma between the name and date of publication.

- One overview of literary theory (Bonnycastle, 2007) has praised "the true and lively spirit of opposition" (p. 204) with which Marxist literary criticism invigorates the discipline.

If the reference does not involve a quotation (as it commonly does not in social science papers), only the date need be given as an in-text citation, provided that the author's name appears in the signal phrase. For paraphrases, APA encourages, though does not require, a page number reference as well. The in-text citation in this case must immediately follow the author's name:

- Bonnycastle (2007) argues that the oppositional tone of Marxist literary criticism invigorates the discipline.

A citation such as this connects to a list of references at the end of the paper. In this case the entry under "References" at the end of the paper would be as follows:

- Bonnycastle, S. (2007). *In search of authority: A guide to literary theory* (3rd ed.). Peterborough, ON: Broadview Press.

Notice here that the date of publication is again foregrounded, appearing immediately after the author's name. Notice too that the formatting of titles differs from that of the MLA style; the details are in sections three and four, below.

2. no signal phrase (or author not named in signal phrase): If the context does not make it clear who the author is, that information must be added to the in-text citation. Note that commas separate the name of the author, the date, and the page number (where this is given):

- Even in recent years some have continued to believe that Marxist literary criticism invigorates the discipline with a "true and lively spirit of opposition" (Bonnycastle, 2005, p. 4).

3. titles of stand-alone works: Stand-alone works are those that are published on their own rather than as part of another work. The titles of stand-alone works (e.g., journals, magazines, newspapers, books, and reports) should be in italics. Writers in the social and behavioural sciences do not normally put the titles of works in the bodies of their papers, but if you do include the title of a stand-alone work, all major words and all words of four letters or more should be capitalized. For book and report titles in the References list, however, capitalize only the first word of the title and subtitle (if any), plus any proper nouns. Journal, magazine, and newspaper titles in the list of References are exceptions; for these, capitalize all major words.

4. **titles of articles and chapters of books**: The titles of these works, and anything else that is published as part of another work, are also not usually mentioned in the body of an essay, though if they are, they should be put in quotation marks, with all major words capitalized. In the References, however, titles of these works should *not* be put in quotation marks or italicized, and no words should be capitalized, with the exception of any proper nouns, and the first word in the title and the first in the subtitle, if any.

5. **placing of in-text citations**: When the author's name appears in a signal phrase, the in-text citation comes directly after the name. Otherwise, the citation follows the paraphrased or quoted material. If a quotation ends with punctuation other than a period or comma, then this should precede the end of the quotation, and a period or comma should still follow the parenthetical reference, if this is grammatically appropriate.

- The claim has been convincingly refuted by Ricks (2010), but it nevertheless continues to be put forward (Dendel, 2013).
- One of Berra's favourite coaching tips was that "ninety per cent of the game is half mental" (Adelman, 2007, p. 98).
- Berra at one point said to his players, "You can observe a lot by watching!" (Adelman, 2007, p. 98).
- Garner (2011) associates statistics and pleasure.

6. **citations when text is in parentheses**: If a parenthetical reference occurs within text in parentheses, commas are used to set off elements of the reference.

- (See Figure 6.1 of Harrison, 2012, for data on transplant waiting lists.)

7. **electronic source—page number unavailable**: If a Web document cited is in PDF format, the page numbers are stable and may be cited as one would the pages of a printed source. The page numbers of many Web sources are unstable, however, and many more lack page numbers altogether. In such cases you should provide a section or paragraph number if a reference is needed. For paragraphs, use the abbreviation "para."

- In a recent Web posting a leading theorist has clearly stated that he finds such an approach "thoroughly objectionable" (Bhabha, 2012, para. 7).
- Bhabha (2012) has clearly stated his opposition to this approach.
- Carter and Zhaba (2009) describe this approach as "more reliable than that adopted by Perkins" (Method section, para. 2).

If you are citing longer texts from electronic versions, chapter references may be more appropriate. For example, if the online Gutenberg edition of Darwin's *On the Origin of Species* were being cited, the citation would be as follows:

- Darwin refers to the core of his theory as an "ineluctable principle" (1856, Chapter 26).

Notice that *chapter* is capitalized and not abbreviated.

Students should be cautioned that online editions of older or classic works are often unreliable; typically there are far more typos and other errors in such versions than there are in print versions. It is often possible to exercise judgement about such matters, however. If, for example, you are not required to base your essay on a particular edition of Darwin's *Origin of Species* but may find your own, you will be far better off using the text you will find on the reputable Project Gutenberg site than you will using a text you might find on a site such as "Manybooks.com."

8. **two or more dates for a work**: If you have consulted a re-issue of a work (whether in printed or electronic form), you should provide both the original date of publication and the date of the re-issue (the date of the version you are using).

- Emerson (1837/1909) asserted that America's "long apprenticeship to the learning of other lands" was "drawing to a close" (para. 1).

The relevant entry in the list of references would look like this:

- Emerson, R. W. (1909). *Essays and English traits*. New York, NY: P. F. Collier & Son. (Original work published 1837)

If you are citing work in a form that has been revised by the author, however, you should cite the date of the revised publication, not the original.

- In a preface to the latest edition of his classic work (2004), Watson discusses its genesis.

9. **multiple authors**: If there are two or three authors, all authors should be named either in the signal phrase or in the in-text citation. Use *and* in the signal phrase but *&* in parentheses.

- Chambliss and Best (2010) have argued that the nature of this research is practical as well as theoretical.
- Two distinguished scholars have argued that the nature of this research is practical as well as theoretical (Chambliss & Best, 2010).

three to five authors: In the body of the text list the names of all authors the first time the work is referred to; for subsequent references use only the first author's name, followed by *et al.* (short for the Latin *et alii*: *and others*).

- Chambliss, Best, Didby, and Jones (2011) have argued that the nature of this research is practical as well as theoretical.
- Four distinguished scholars have argued that the nature of this research is practical as well as theoretical (Chambliss, Best, Didby, & Jones, 2011).

more than five authors: Use only the first author's name, followed by *et al.* (short for the Latin *et alii*: *and others*).

- Chambliss et al. (2011) have argued that the nature of this research is practical as well as theoretical.
- Six distinguished scholars have argued that the nature of this research is practical as well as theoretical (Chambliss et al., 2011).

10. **corporate author**: As you would with an individual human author, provide the name of a corporate author either in the body of your text or in a parenthetical citation. Recommended practice is to provide the full name of an organization on the first occasion, followed by an abbreviation, and then to use the abbreviation for subsequent references:

- Blindness has decreased markedly but at an uneven pace since the late 1800s (National Institute for the Blind [NIB], 2002).

11. **author not given**: If the author of the source is not given, it may be identified in the parenthetical reference by a short form of the title.

- Confusion over voting reform is widespread ("Results of National Study," 2012).

12. **date not given**: Some sources, particularly electronic ones, do not provide a date of publication. Where this is the case, use the abbreviation *n.d.* for *no date*.

- Some still claim that evidence of global climate change is difficult to come by (Sanders, n.d.; Zimmerman, 2012).

13. **two or more works in the same citation**: In this case, the works should appear in in-text citations in the same order they do in the list of references. If the works are by different authors, arrange the sources alphabetically by author's last name and separate the citations with a semicolon. If the works are by the same authors, arrange the sources by publication date. Add *a*, *b*, *c*, etc. after the year to distinguish works written by the same authors in the same year.

APA Style

- Various studies have established a psychological link between fear and sexual arousal (Aikens, Cox, & Bartlett, 1998; Looby & Cairns, 2008).
- Various studies appear to have established a psychological link between fear and sexual arousal (Looby & Cairns, 1999, 2002, 2005).
- Looby and Cairns (1999a, 1999b, 2002, 2005a, 2005b) have investigated extensively the link between fear and sexual arousal.

14. **two or more authors with the same last name**: If the References list includes two or more authors with the same last name, the in-text citation should supply an initial:

- One of the leading economists of the time advocated wage and price controls (H. Johnston, 1977).

15. **works in a collection of readings or anthology**: In the in-text citation for a work in an anthology or collection of readings, use the name of the author of the work, not that of the editor of the anthology. If the work was first published in the collection you have consulted, there is only the one date to cite. But if the work is reprinted in that collection after having first been published elsewhere, cite the date of the original publication and the date of the collection you have consulted, separating these dates with a slash. The following citation refers to an article by Frederic W. Gleach that was first published in a collection of readings edited by Jennifer Brown and Elizabeth Vibert.

- One of the essays in Brown and Vibert's collection argues that we should rethink the Pocahontas myth (Gleach, 1996).

In your list of references, this work should be alphabetized under Gleach, the author of the piece you have consulted, not under Brown.

The next example is a lecture by Georg Simmel first published in 1903, which a student consulted in an edited collection by Roberta Garner that was published in 2001.

- Simmel (1903/2001) argues that the "deepest problems of modern life derive from the claim of the individual to preserve the autonomy and individuality of his existence" (p. 141).

The reference list entry would look like this:

Simmel, G. (2001). The metropolis and mental life. In R. Garner (Ed.), *Social theory—Continuity and confrontation: A reader* (pp. 141–153). Peterborough, ON: Broadview Press. (Original work published in 1903)

As you can see, in your reference list these works are listed under the authors of the pieces (Gleach or Simmel), not under the compilers, editors, or translators of the collection (Brown & Vibert or Garner). If you cite another work by a different author from the same anthology or book of readings, that should appear as a separate entry in your list of references—again, alphabetized under the author's name.

16. **indirect source**: If you are citing a source from a reference other than the source itself, you should use the phrase "as cited in" in your in-text citation.

- In de Beauvoir's famous phrase, "one is not born a woman, one becomes one" (as cited in Levey, 2001, para. 3).

In this case, the entry in your reference list would be for Levey, not de Beauvoir.

17. **private and personal communications**: Since the list of references should include only sources that your readers can access themselves, it should not include personal, private, and undocumented or unarchived communications, whether these are by telephone, written letter, e-mail, or other means. Cite these communications only in your text. Provide the initials and surname of the person you communicated with as well as the date of communication.

- K. Montegna (personal communication, January 21, 2013) has expressed skepticism over this method's usefulness.

O *About References*

The list of references in APA style is an alphabetized listing of sources that appears at the end of an essay, article, or book. Usually, it includes all the information necessary to identify and retrieve each of the sources you have cited, and only the works you have cited. In this case the list is entitled *References*. If the list includes all works you have consulted, regardless of whether or not you have cited them, it should be entitled *Bibliography*. The list of references should include only sources that can be accessed by your readers, and so it should not include private communication, such as private letters, memos, e-mail messages, and telephone or personal conversations. Those should be cited only in your text (see the section above).

Entries should be ordered alphabetically by author surname, or, if there is no known author, by title. The first line of each entry should be flush with the left-hand margin, with all subsequent lines indented about one half inch. Double-space throughout the list of references.

The basic format for all entries is author (if available), date (give *n.d.* if there is no date), title, and publication information. Remember that one function of the list of references is to provide the information your readers need if they wish to locate your sources for themselves; APA allows any "non-routine" information that could assist in identifying the sources to be added in square brackets to any entry (e.g., [Sunday business section], [Motion picture], [Interview with O. Sacks]).

In the References examples that follow, information about entries for electronic sources has been presented in an integrated fashion alongside information about referencing sources in other media, such as print, film, and so on. Whenever you are required to give a website URL that does not all fit on one line, do not insert a hyphen; break the URL before a slash or period (with the exception of the slashes in *http://*).

18. **book with single author**: For a work with one author the entry should begin with the last name, followed by a comma, and then the author's initials as applicable, followed by the date of publication in parentheses. Note that initials are generally used rather than first names, even when authors are identified by first name in the work itself. For publishers in North America, give the city and an abbreviation of the state or province of publication; give the city and country for works published elsewhere. Leave out abbreviations such as *Inc.* and *Co.* in publisher's names but keep *Press* and *Books*.

Gee, J. P. (2012). *Social linguistics and literacies: Ideology in discourses* (4th ed.). London, England: Routledge.

19. **two to seven authors**: Last names should in all cases come first, followed by initials. Use commas to separate the authors' names, and use an ampersand rather than *and* before the last author. Note that the authors' names should appear in the order they are listed; sometimes this is not alphabetical.

Eagles, M., Bickerton, J. P., & Gagnon, A. (1991). *The almanac of Canadian politics*. Peterborough, ON: Broadview Press.

20. **more than seven authors**: List the names of the first six authors, add an ellipsis, and then give the last author's name.

Newsome, M. R., Scheibel, R. S., Hanten, G., Chu, Z., Steinberg, J. L., Hunter, J. V. ... Levin, H. S. (2010). Brain activation while thinking about the self from another person's perspective after traumatic brain injury in adolescents. *Neuropsychology, 24*(2), 139–147.

21. **corporate author**: If a work has been issued by a government body, a corporation, or some other organization and no author is identified, the entry should be listed by the name of the group. If this group is also the work's publisher, write *Author* where the publisher's name would normally go.

Broadview Press. (2005). *Annual report*. Calgary, AB: Author.

Broadview Press. (n.d.). Questions and answers about book pricing. Broadview Press Web Site. Retrieved from www.broadviewpress.com/bookpricing.asp?inc=bookpricing

City of Toronto, City Planning Division. (2000, June). *Toronto at the crossroads: Shaping our future*. Toronto, ON: Author.

22. works with unknown author: Works with an unknown author should be alphabetized by title.

> *Columbia encyclopedia* (6th ed.). (2001). New York, NY: Columbia University Press.

If you have referred to only one entry in an encyclopedia or dictionary, however, the entry in your list of references should be by the title of that entry (see below).

23. two or more works by the same author: The author's name should appear for all entries. Entries should be ordered by year of publication.

> Menand, L. (2002). *The metaphysical club: A story of ideas in America.* New York, NY: Knopf.
> Menand, L. (2004, June 28). Bad comma: Lynne Truss's strange grammar [Review of the book *Eats, shoots & leaves*]. *The New Yorker.* Retrieved from http://www .newyorker.com

If two or more cited works by the same author have been published in the same year, arrange these alphabetically and use letters to distinguish among them: (2011a), (2011b), and so on.

24. edited works: Entries for edited works include the abbreviation *Ed.* or *Eds.* The second example below is for a book with both an author and an editor; since the original work in this entry was published earlier than the present edition, that information is given in parentheses at the end.

> Gross, B., Field, D., & Pinker, L. (Eds.). (2002). *New approaches to the history of psychoanalysis.* New York, NY: Duckworth.

APA Style

Sapir, E. (1981). *Selected writings in language, culture, and personality*. D. G. Mandelbaum (Ed.). Berkeley, CA: University of California Press. (Original work published 1949)

25. works with an author and a translator: The translator's name, along with the designation *Trans.*, is included in parentheses after the title; the original publication date is given in parentheses following the present edition's publication information.

Jung, C. G. (2006). *The undiscovered self* (R. F. C. Hull, Trans.). New York, NY: Signet. (Original work published 1959)

26. selections from anthologies or collections of readings: A selection from a collection of readings or an anthology should be listed as follows:

Gleach, F. W. (1996). Controlled speculation: Interpreting the saga of Pocahontas and Captain John Smith. In J. Brown & E. Vibert (Eds.), *Reading beyond words: Contexts for Native history* (pp. 21–42). Peterborough, ON: Broadview.

Rosengarten, H. (2002). Fleiss's nose and Freud's mind: A new perspective. In B. Gross, D. Field, & L. Pinker (Eds.), *New approaches to the history of psychoanalysis* (pp. 232–243). New York, NY: Duckworth.

Taylor, E. (1992). Biological consciousness and the experience of the transcendent: William James and American functional psychology. In R. H. Wozniak (Ed.), *Mind and body: René Descartes to William James*. Retrieved from http://serendip.brynmawr.edu /Mind/James.html

27. electronic version of a print book: Give the site's URL in the place where publication information would normally go.

> Bailey, K. D. (1994). *Sociology and the new systems theory: Toward a theoretical synthesis*. Retrieved from https://play.google.com/

28. journal articles: Notice that article titles are not enclosed in quotation marks, and that both the journal title and the volume number are in italics. If all issues of a given volume of a journal begin with page 1, include the issue number as well, directly after the volume number, in parentheses and not italicized. For online journal articles, you should also include the digital object identifier (DOI): a string of numbers, letters, and punctuation, beginning with *10*, usually located on the first or copyright page. If no DOI is available, you should include the URL for the journal's homepage.

> Barker, P. (2004). The impact of class size on the classroom behaviour of special needs students: A longitudinal study. *Educational Quarterly, 25*(4), 87–99.
>
> Best, R. K. (2012). Disease politics and medical research funding: Three ways advocacy shapes policy. *American Sociological Review, 77*, 780–803. Retrieved from http://asr.sagepub.com/
>
> Laughlin, C. D., & Tiberia, V. A. (2012). Archetypes: Toward a Jungian anthropology of consciousness. *Anthropology of Consciousness, 23*, 127–157. doi:10.1111/j.1556-3537.2012.01063.x
>
> Surtees, P. (2008). The psychology of the children's crusade of 1212. *Studies in Medieval History and Society, 3*(4), 279–325. doi:10.1008/smhs.2008.0581

APA Style

29. **abstract of a journal article**: Cite as you would the journal article itself, adding *Abstract* in square brackets.

> Laughlin, C. D., & Tiberia, V. A. (2012). Archetypes: Toward a Jungian anthropology of consciousness [Abstract]. *Anthropology of Consciousness, 23*, 127–157. doi:10.1111/j.1556-3537.2012.01063.x

30. **magazine articles**: The basic principles are the same as for journal articles. Note that neither quotation marks nor italics are used for the titles of articles. If no author is identified, the title of the article should appear first. For monthly magazines, provide the month as well as the year; for magazines issued more frequently, give the day, month, and year. Include the homepage URL for magazine articles online.

> Dyer, A. (2012, November/December). The end of the world … again. *SkyNews, 18*(4), 38–39.
> The rise of the yuan: Turning from green to red. (2012, October 20). *The Economist, 405*(42), 67–68.
> Steavenson, W. (2012, November 12). Two revolutions: Women in the new Egypt. *The New Yorker, 88*(35), 32–38. Retrieved from http://www.newyorker.com

31. **newspaper articles**: The basic principles to follow with newspaper articles or editorials are the same as with magazine articles (see above), but volume and issue numbers are not included, and page numbers are preceded by *p.* or *pp.* APA requires that all page numbers for print versions be provided when articles do not continue on consecutive pages. Notice that if there is no letter assigned to a newspaper section, you should give the section's title in square brackets.

Bennett, J. (2012, December 16). How to attack the gender pay gap? *The New York Times* [Sunday business section], pp. 1, 6.

Gray, J. (2012, December 20). Stepping into the proxy frays. *The Globe and Mail*, p. B6.

If you are citing an online version of a newspaper article you have retrieved through a search of its website, you should provide the URL for the site, not for the exact location of the article. Since the online version of the article in the example below does not have page numbers, none are included in the References entry.

Gray, J. (2012, December 20). Stepping into the proxy frays. *The Globe and Mail*. Retrieved from http://www .globeandmail.com

32. **book reviews**: The name of the reviewer (if it has been provided) should come first, followed by the date and title of the review, and the information on the book itself, as follows:

Tavris, C. (2012, April 25). Psychology and its discontents. [Review of the book *Psychology's ghosts: The crisis in the profession and the way back*, by J. Kagan]. *Wall Street Journal*. Retrieved from http://online.wsj.com/article /SB1000142405270230453790457727776026027611 48.html

33. **reference work entries**: List by the author of the entry, if known; otherwise, list by the entry itself.

Lister, M. (1999). Consumers' Association of Canada. *The Canadian encyclopedia* (Year 2000 ed.). Toronto, ON: McClelland & Stewart.

Saint Lawrence Seaway. (2001). *The Columbia encyclopedia* (6th ed.). Retrieved from http://www.bartleby.com/65 /st/STLawrSwy.html

34. films and video recordings: Begin entries for motion pictures with the names of the producers and director, followed by the date of release, the film's title, the medium in square brackets, the location of origin, and the name of the studio.

Ball, C. J., Ryder, A., Tyrer, W., Dysinger, E., Todd, J., Todd, S., Thomas, E. (Producers), & Nolan, C. (Director). (2000). *Memento* [Blu-ray disc]. United States: New-market Films.

Egoyan, A., Weiss, J., Vroll, S., Iron, D. (Producers), & Polley, S. (Director). (2006). *Away from her* [Motion picture]. Canada: Lionsgate Films.

35. episodes from television series: Entries for television show episodes should begin with the names of the writer and director, followed by the date, episode title, medium, producer's name, series title, location, and production company's name. Identify the role, in parentheses, of each person listed.

Weiner, M. (Writer), & Getzinger, J. (Director). (2012). A little kiss [Television series episode]. In M. Weiner (Executive producer), *Mad men*. Santa Monica, CA: Lionsgate Television.

36. podcasts: Use the entry for a television series episode as a model, giving the type of podcast as the medium, and adding the website's URL. Give the full date of the original broadcast.

Eisen, J. (Writer). (2010, May 17–31). Have your meat and eat it too! Parts 1–3. [Audio podcast]. In L. Noth (Producer), *CBC ideas*. Retrieved from http://www.cbc.ca/ideas/episodes/2010/05/17/have-your-meat-and-eat-it-too-part-1-2-listen/

37. music recordings: Arrange an entry for a music recording as follows: give the writer's name, the copyright date of the piece of music, its title, the album title, the medium in square brackets, the place of origin, and the label name. If the piece is recorded by someone other than the writer, note that in square brackets after the piece's title. Add the recording date at the end of the entry if it differs from the copyright date.

Berlin, I. (1935). Cheek to cheek [Recorded by J. Pass]. On *Blues for Fred* [CD]. Berkeley, CA: Pablo Records. (1988, February 3).

Waits, T. (1999). Eyeball kid. On *Mule Variations* [CD]. Los Angeles, CA: Anti.

38. interviews: How you format an entry for an interview will depend on where it is located. If you watched or listened to a recording of the interview, use the format appropriate to the medium. The second example below is for an interview of Jane Goodall on the television program *Bill Moyers Journal*, which was accessed online as a video webcast. Notice that the interviewee's name comes first, and that the entry is formatted in the same way as an entry for a television series episode that is available online. The first example is for an interview with Willie Nelson printed in a periodical. Here, the entry follows the format for a newspaper article, with the interviewer in the author position, and information about the interviewee in square brackets. Notice as well that, although the periodical is called a magazine, this publication goes by date only, not volume and issue number, and so the newspaper article format is the appropriate choice. These guidelines apply only to published interviews; unpublished interviews you have conducted yourself are considered private correspondence and should not be included in your References list.

Goldman, A. (2012, December 16). The silver-headed stranger [Interview with W. Nelson]. *New York Times Magazine*, p. 12.

Goodall, J. (2009, November 27). Interview by B. Moyers. In G. Ablow, W. Brangham, P. Meryash, B. Rate, & C. White (Producers), *Bill Moyers journal* [Video webcast]. Retrieved from http://www.pbs.org/moyers/journal/11272009/watch1.html

39. **documents on a website**: Give the author's name and date, if available (use *n.d.* for no date), the work's title, and the retrieval information.

LePan, D. (n.d.) The psychology of skyscrapers. Retrieved from http://donlepan.com

40. **blog posts**: Start with the writer's name; then give the full date, entry title, blog title, and retrieval information.

Gautam, S. (2012, July 22). Structure of childhood temperaments. *The mouse trap*. Retrieved from http://the-mouse-trap.com/2012/07/22/structure-of-childhood-temperaments/#comment-6470

41. **entries in a wiki**: Because wikis can be revised by anyone, their content tends to change over time. It is important, therefore, to include your date of access in the References entry. Wiki entries often have no single date of publication; if that's the case, use *n.d.*

> Code-switching. (n.d.). In *Wikipedia*. Retrieved January 17, 2013, from http://en.wikipedia.org/wiki/Code_switching

42. **tweets**: If the author's real name is known, provide it first, followed by the author's screen name in square brackets. If the author's real name cannot be determined, provide only the screen name, without the square brackets. Include only the date, not the time, of posting, and add *Twitter post* in square brackets. Include the entire tweet.

> Welch, J. [jack_welch]. (2012, October 5). Unbelievable jobs numbers..these Chicago guys will do anything.. can't debate so change numbers [Twitter post]. Retrieved from http://twitter.com/jack_welch

43. **other Web references**: In the case of online sources not covered by the above, the same basic principles apply. Where an author or editor is indicated, list by author; otherwise, list by title. If the source is undated or its content likely to change, you should include the date on which you accessed the material. Use square brackets to include information that will help identify the source.

> Brown University. (2006, May). Brown University. Women writers project. Retrieved February 28, 2013, from http://www.brown.edu/

44. **maps or charts**: Include the medium in square brackets.

> Profile of book publishing and exclusive agency, for English language firms [Chart]. (2012). Statistics Canada. Retrieved from http://www.statcan.ca/english/pgdb /arts02.htm

O *APA Style Sample*

Following is a sample of text with citations in APA style. Note that a sample essay in APA style is included at the end of this book.

Urban renewal is as much a matter of psychology as it is of bricks and mortar. As Goldberger (2005) notes, there have been many plans to revitalize Havana. But both that city and the community of Cuban exiles in Florida remain haunted by a sense of separation. As Lourdes Casal (1998) reminds us, exile "is living where there is no house whatever in which we were ever children" (l. 2–3).

The psychology of outsiders also makes a difference. Part of the reason Americans have not much noticed the dire plight of their fifth-largest city is that it does not "stir the national imagination" (Rybczynski, 1998, p. 12). Conversely, there has been far more concern over the state of cities such as New Orleans and Quebec, whose history and architecture excite the romantic imagination. As Nora Phelps (1998) has discussed, the past is in itself a trigger for romantic notions, and it is inevitable that cities whose history is particularly visible will engender passionate attachments. And as Stephanie Wright and Carole King (2012) have detailed in an important study, almost all French-speaking Quebecers feel their heritage to be bound up with that of Quebec City. (Richard Ford's character Frank Bascombe has suggested that "New Orleans defeats itself" by longing "for a mystery it doesn't have and never will, if it ever did" [Ford, 1995, p. 48] but this remains a minority view.)

Georgiana Gibson (2011a) is also among those who have investigated the interplay between urban psychology and urban reality. Gibson's personal website (2011b) now includes the first of a set of working models she is developing in an attempt to represent the effects of psychological schemata on the landscape.

APA Style

The in-text citations above would connect to References as follows:

References

Casal, L. (1998, January 26). Definition. (E. Macklin, Trans.). *The New Yorker*, 79.

Ford, R. (1995). *The sportswriter* (2nd ed.). New York, NY: Random House.

Gibson, G. (2011a). *Cities in the twentieth century*. Boston, MA: Beacon.

Gibson, G. (2011b, June 10). Homepage. Retrieved from http://www.geography.byu.edu/GIBSON/personal.htm

Goldberger, P. (2005, January 26). Annals of preservation: Bringing back Havana. *The New Yorker*, 50–62. Retrieved from http://www.newyorker.com

Phelps, N. (1998). Pastness and the foundations of romanticism. *Romanticism on the Net, 11*. doi:10.1008/rotn.1998.4611

Rybczynski, W. (1998, February 5). The fifth city. [Review of the book *A prayer for the city*]. *The New York Review of Books*, 12–14.

Wright, S., & King, C. (2012). *Quebec: A history* (Vols. 1–2). Montreal, QC: McGill-Queen's University Press.

Among the details to notice in this reference system:

- Where two or more works by the same author are included in References, they are ordered by date of publication.
- APA style prefers author initials rather than first names.
- Only the first words of titles and subtitles are capitalized, except for proper nouns.
- The date appears in parentheses near the beginning of each entry in References.
- The in-text citation comes directly after the name of the author or after the end quotation mark. Often, these citations fall just before the period or comma in the surrounding sentence.
- If an in-text citation occurs within text in parentheses, commas are used to set off elements of the reference.
- When a work has appeared in an edited collection, information on the editors must be included in the reference.
- Authors' first and last names are reversed; note the use of the ampersand (&) between author names.
- Translators should be included under References.
- Publisher as well as city of publication, including abbreviations for all states and provinces, should be given.
- Months and publisher names are not abbreviated; the day of the month follows the name of the month.
- Online references include the date of publication or of last revision in parentheses immediately after the author's name, and the date of access, which appears within a phrase near the end of the entry, e.g., "Retrieved July 6, 2013, from http://www.broadviewpress.com": note that, if a URL ends a reference entry, there is no period at the end of the entry.

APA Style

Chicago Style

◉ Chicago Style

○ *About Chicago Style*

The University of Chicago's massively comprehensive *Chicago Manual of Style* (16th edition, 2010), provides full information on two documentation systems: an author-date system of citation that is similar to APA style, and a traditional foot- or endnoting system. The latter, which this book refers to as Chicago Style, and which is often used in the history and philosophy disciplines, is outlined below. This chapter also includes, at the end, a short essay excerpt using Chicago Style documentation. Full sample essays in Chicago Style are available on the Broadview website. Go to sites.broadviewpress.com/writing/. You can also find additional information at Chicago Style's online site (www.chicagomanualofstyle.org).

In the pages that follow, information about electronic sources has been presented in an integrated fashion, with information about referencing hard copies of print sources presented alongside information about referencing online versions. General guidelines covering entries for online sources are as follows. Begin each note and bibliography entry for an electronic source as you would for a non-electronic source, including all relevant publication information that the source makes available. Then provide either the website's URL, followed by the usual end punctuation for the note or entry, or, if available, the source's digital object identifier (DOI): a string of numbers, letters, and punctuation, beginning with 10, usually located on the first or copyright page. If both a URL and DOI are available, provide only the latter; DOIs are preferred because they are stable links to sources, whereas URLs are often not permanent. If you need to break a URL or DOI over two or more lines, do not insert any hyphens at the break point; instead, break after a colon or double slash or before other marks of punctuation. Note that Chicago Style does not put angle brackets around URLs. Except when there is no publication or modification date available, Chicago Style does not require the addition of access dates for online material, but your instructors may wish you to include them. If so, put them after the URL or DOI, after the word *accessed*.

1. **notes:** The basic principle of Chicago Style is to create a note each time one cites a source. The note can appear at the foot of the page on which the citation is made, or it can be part of a separate list, titled *Notes*, situated at the end of the essay and before the bibliography. For both foot- and endnotes, a superscript number at the end of the clause in which the reference appears points to the relevant note:

- Bonnycastle refers to "the true and lively spirit of opposition" with which Marxist literary criticism invigorates the discipline.[1]

The superscript number [1] here is linked to the information provided where the same number appears at either the foot of the page or in the list of notes at the end of the main text of the paper:

   1. Stephen Bonnycastle, *In Search of Authority: An Introductory Guide to Literary Theory*, 3rd ed. (Peterborough, ON: Broadview Press, 2007), 204.

Notice that the author's name is in the normal order, elements of the note are separated by commas, publication information is in parentheses, and the first line of the note is indented. The note ends with a page number for the citation.

In addition, all works cited, as well as works that have been consulted but are not cited in the body of your essay, must be included in an alphabetically arranged list, titled *Bibliography*, that appears at the end of the essay. The entry there would in this case be as follows:

Bonnycastle, Stephen. *In Search of Authority: An Introductory Guide to Literary Theory.* 3rd ed. Peterborough, ON: Broadview Press, 2007.

In the entry in the bibliography, notice that the author's name is inverted, elements of the entry are separated by periods, and no parentheses are placed around the publication information. Also, the entry is given a hanging indent: the first line is flush with the left-hand margin, and subsequent lines are indented. Notice as well that the province or state of publication is included in both notes and bibliography entries if the city of publication is not widely known.

In the various examples that follow, note formats and bibliography entry formats for each kind of source are shown together.

2. **titles: italics/quotation marks:** Notice in the above example that both the title and the subtitle are in italics. Titles of short works (such as articles, poems, and short stories) should be put in quotation marks. In all titles key words should be capitalized. For more details, see the Title of Source section in the chapter on MLA documentation above.

3. **multiple references to the same work:** For later notes referencing an already-cited source, use the author's last name, title (in shortened form if it is over four words long), and page number only.

> 1. Bonnycastle, *In Search of Authority*, 28.

If successive references are to the same work, use *ibid.* (an abbreviation of the Latin *ibidem*, meaning *in the same place*) instead of repeating information that appears in the previous note.

> 1. Sean Carver, "The Economic Foundations for Unrest in East Timor, 1970–1995," *Journal of Economic History* 21, no. 2 (2011): 103.
>
> 2. Ibid., 109.
>
> 3. Ibid., 111.
>
> 4. Jennifer Riley, "East Timor in the Pre-Independence Years," *Asian History Online* 11, no. 4 (2012): par. 18, http://www.aho.ubc.edu/prs/text-only/issue.45/16.3jr.txt.
>
> 5. Ibid., par. 24.

> Carver, Sean. "The Economic Foundations for Unrest in East Timor, 1970–1995." *Journal of Economic History* 21, no. 2 (2011): 100–121.
>
> Riley, Jennifer. "East Timor in the Pre-Independence Years." *Asian History Online* 11, no. 4 (2012). http://www.aho.ubc.edu/prs/text-only/issue.45/16.3jr.txt.

4. **page number or date unavailable:** If an Internet document cited is in PDF format, the page numbers are stable and may be cited in the same way that one would the pages of a printed book or journal article. Many Internet page numbers are unstable, however, and many more lack page

numbers. Instead, provide a section number, paragraph number, or other identifier if available.

2. Hanif Bhabha, "Family Life in 1840s Virginia," *Southern History Web Archives* 45, no. 3 (2013): par. 14. http://shweb.ut.edu/history/american.nineteenthc/bhabha.html (accessed March 3, 2009).

Bhabha, Hanif. "Family Life in 1840s Virginia." *Southern History Web Archives* 45, no. 3 (2013). http://shweb.ut.edu/history/american.nineteenthc/bhabha.html.

If you are citing longer texts from electronic versions, and counting paragraph numbers is impracticable, chapter references may be more appropriate. For example, if the online Gutenberg edition of Darwin's *On the Origin of Species* were being cited, the citation would be as follows:

- Darwin refers to the core of his theory as an "ineluctable principle."[1]

1. Charles Darwin, *On the Origin of Species* (1856; Project Gutenberg, 2001), chap. 26, http://www.gutenberg.darwin.origin.frrp.ch26.html.

Darwin, Charles. *On the Origin of Species*. 1856. Project Gutenberg, 2001. http://www.gutenberg.darwin.origin.frrp.ch26.html.

Students should be cautioned that online editions of older or classic works are often unreliable; typically there are far more typos and other errors in online versions of literary texts than there are in print versions. It is often possible to exercise judgement about such matters, however. If, for example, you are not required to base your essay on a particular edition of Darwin's *Origin of Species* but may find your own, you will be far better off using the text you will find on the reputable Project Gutenberg site than you will using a text you might find on a site such as "Manybooks. com."

When there is no date for a source, include *n. d.*, as in the first example below. When there is no date for an online source, include your access date.

> 1. Thomas Gray, *Gray's Letters*, vol. 1 (London: John Sharpe, n. d.), 60.
>
> 2. Don LePan, *Skyscraper Art*, http://www.donlepan.com /Skyscraper_Art.html (accessed February 10, 2013).

> Gray, Thomas. *Gray's Letters*. Vol. 1. London: John Sharpe, n. d.
> LePan, Don. *Skyscraper Art*. http://www.donlepan.com /Skyscraper_Art.html (accessed February 10, 2013).

5. **two or more dates for a work**: Note that in the Darwin example above both the date of the original publication and the date of the modern edition are provided. If you are citing work in a form that has been revised by the author, however, you should cite the date of the revised publication, not the original, and use the abbreviation *rev. ed.* to indicate that the work has been revised.

> 1. Eric Foner, *Free Soil, Free Labor, Free Men: A Study of Antebellum America*, rev. ed. (New York: Oxford University Press, 1999), 178.

> Foner, Eric. *Free Soil, Free Labor, Free Men: A Study of Antebellum America*. Rev. ed. New York: Oxford University Press, 1999.

6. **two or three authors**: If there are two or three authors, they should be identified as follows in the footnote and in the Bibliography. Pay attention to where commas do and do not appear, and note that in the Bibliography entry, only the first author's name is inverted. Put the names of the authors in the order in which they appear in the work itself.

> 4. Eric Alderman and Mark Green, *Tony Blair and the Rise of New Labour* (London: Cassell, 2002), 180.

> Alderman, Eric, and Mark Green. *Tony Blair and the Rise of New Labour*. London: Cassell, 2002.

7. **four or more authors**: In the footnote name only the first author, and use the phrase *et al.*, an abbreviation of the Latin *et alii*, meaning *and others*. In the bibliography name all authors, as below:

> 11. Victoria Fromkin et al., *An Introduction to Language*, 4th Canadian ed. (Toronto: Nelson, 2010), 113.

> Fromkin, Victoria, Robert Rodman, Nina Hyams, and Kirsten M. Hummel. *An Introduction to Language*. 4th Canadian ed. Toronto: Nelson, 2010.

8. **author unknown / corporate author / government document**: Identify by the corporate author if known, and otherwise by the title of the work. Unsigned newspaper articles or dictionary and encyclopedia entries are usually not listed in the bibliography. In notes, unsigned dictionary or encyclopedia entries are identified by the title of the reference work, e.g., *Columbia Encyclopedia*, and unsigned newspaper articles are listed by the title of the article in footnotes but by the title of the newspaper in the bibliography. Ignore initial articles (the, a, an) when alphabetizing.

6. *National Hockey League Guide, 1966–67* (Toronto: National Hockey League, 1966), 77.

7. "Argentina's President Calls on UK Prime Minister to Relinquish Control of Falkland Islands," *Vancouver Sun*, January 3, 2013, A9.

8. Broadview Press, "Questions and Answers about Book Pricing," Broadview Press, http://www.broadviewpress.com /bookpricing.asp?inc=bookpricing (accessed January 18, 2013).

9. Commonwealth of Massachusetts, *Records of the Transportation Inquiry, 2004* (Boston: Massachusetts Publishing Office, 2005), 488.

10. *Columbia Encyclopedia*, "Ecuador," http://bartleby.com .columbia.txt.acc.html (accessed February 4, 2013).

11. U.S. Congress. House Committee on Ways and Means, Subcommittee on Trade, *Free Trade Area of the Americas: Hearings*, 105th Cong., 1st sess., July 22, 1997, Hearing Print 105–32, 160, http://www.waysandmeans.house.gov /hearings.asp (accessed January 22, 2013).

Following are the bibliography entries for the preceding notes (notice that, because unsigned newspaper articles and articles from well-known reference works are not usually included in Chicago Style bibliographies, the *Vancouver Sun* and *Columbia Encyclopedia* articles are not included):

Broadview Press. "Questions and Answers about Book Pricing." Broadview Press. http://www.broadviewpress.com /bookpricing.asp?inc=bookpricing (accessed January 18, 2013).

Commonwealth of Massachusetts. *Records of the Transportation Inquiry, 2004.* Boston: Massachusetts Publishing Office, 2005.

National Hockey League Guide, 1966–67. Toronto: National
    Hockey League, 1966.
U.S. Congress. House Committee on Ways and Means. Sub-
    committee on Trade. *Free Trade Area of the Americas:*
    Hearing before the Subcommittee on Trade. 105th Cong.,
    1st sess., July 22, 1997. Hearing Print 105–32. http://
    www.waysandmeans.house.gov/hearings.asp (accessed
    January 22, 2013).

9. **works from a collection of readings or anthology**: In the
citation for a work in an anthology or collection of essays,
use the name of the author of the work you are citing. If
the work is reprinted in one source but was first published
elsewhere, include the details of the original publication in
the bibliography.

    6. Eric Hobsbawm, "Peasant Land Occupations," in
Uncommon People: Resistance and Rebellion (London: Wei-
denfeld & Nicolson, 1998), 167.
    7. Frederic W. Gleach, "Controlled Speculation: Inter-
preting the Saga of Pocahontas and Captain John Smith," in
Reading Beyond Words: Contexts for Native History, 2nd ed.,
ed. Jennifer Brown and Elizabeth Vibert (Peterborough, ON:
Broadview Press, 2003), 43.

Gleach, Frederic W. "Controlled Speculation: Interpreting
    the Saga of Pocahontas and Captain John Smith." In
    Reading Beyond Words: Contexts for Native History, 2nd
    ed., edited by Jennifer Brown and Elizabeth Vibert,
    39–74. Peterborough, ON: Broadview Press, 2003.
Hobsbawm, Eric. "Peasant Land Occupations." In *Uncom-*
    mon People: Resistance and Rebellion, 166–90. London:
    Weidenfeld & Nicolson, 1998. Originally published in
    Past and Present 62 (1974): 120–52.

10. **indirect source**: If you are citing a source from a reference other than the source itself, you should include information about both sources, supplying as much information as you are able to about the original source.

- In de Beauvoir's famous phrase, "one is not born a woman, one becomes one."[1]

1. Simone de Beauvoir, *The Second Sex* (London: Heinemann, 1966), 44, quoted in Ann Levey, "Feminist Philosophy Today," *Philosophy Now*, par. 8, http://www.ucalgary.ca.philosophy.nowsite675.html (accessed February 4, 2013).

de Beauvoir, Simone. *The Second Sex*. London: Heinemann, 1966. Quoted in Ann Levey, "Feminist Philosophy Today," *Philosophy Now*, http://www.ucalgary.ca.philosophy.nowsite675.html (accessed February 4, 2013).

11. **two or more works by the same author**: After the first entry in the bibliography, use three hyphens to begin subsequent entries of works by the same author (rather than repeat the author's name). Entries for multiple works by the same author are normally arranged alphabetically by title.

Menand, Louis. "Bad Comma: Lynne Truss's Strange Grammar." *The New Yorker*, June 28, 2004. http://www.newyorker.com/critics/books/?040628crbo_books1.
---. *The Metaphysical Club: A Story of Ideas in America*. New York: Knopf, 2002.

12. **edited works**: Entries for edited works include the abbreviation *ed.* or *eds.* Note that when *ed.* appears after a title, it means "edited by."

5. Brian Gross, ed., *New Approaches to Environmental Politics: A Survey* (New York: Duckworth, 2004), 177.

6. Mary Shelley, *Frankenstein*, 2nd ed., ed. Lorne Macdonald and Kathleen Scherf, Broadview Editions (1818; Peterborough, ON: Broadview Press, 2001), 89.

Gross, Brian, ed. *New Approaches to Environmental Politics: A Survey*. New York: Duckworth, 2004.

Shelley, Mary. *Frankenstein*. 2nd ed. Edited by Lorne Macdonald and Kathleen Scherf. Broadview Editions. Peterborough, ON: Broadview, 2001. First published in 1818.

13. **translated works**: The name of the translator follows the work's title. Notice that, in the first example below, the work's author is unknown; begin with the author's name if it is known.

1. *Beowulf*, trans. R. M. Liuzza, 2nd ed. (Peterborough, ON: Broadview, 2012), 91.

2. Franz Kafka, "A Hunger Artist," *The Metamorphosis and Other Stories*, trans. Ian Johnston (Peterborough, ON: Broadview, 2015), 112.

Beowulf. Translated by R. M. Liuzza. 2nd ed. Peterborough, ON: Broadview, 2012.

Kafka, Franz. "A Hunger Artist." *The Metamorphosis and Other Stories*. Translated by Ian Johnston. Peterborough, ON: Broadview, 2015.

14. **e-books**: Electronic books come in several formats. The first of the two sample citations below is for a book found online; the second is for a book downloaded onto an e-reader.

4. Mary Roberts Rinehart, *Tish* (1916; Project Gutenberg, 2005), chap. 2, http://www.gutenberg.org/catalog/world/readfile?fk_files=1452441.

5. Lao Tzu, *Tao Te Ching: A Book about the Way and the Power of the Way*, trans. Ursula K. Le Guin (Boston: Shambhala, 2011), iBook Reader e-book, verse 12.

Lao Tzu. *Tao Te Ching: A Book about the Way and the Power of the Way*. Translated by Ursula K. Le Guin. Boston: Shambhala, 2011. iBook Reader e-book.

Rinehart, Mary Roberts. *Tish*. 1916. Project Gutenberg, 2005. http://www.gutenberg.org/catalog/world/readfile?fk_files=1452441.

15. **magazine articles**: The titles of articles appear in quotation marks. The page range should appear in the bibliography if it is known. (This will not always be possible if the source is an electronic version.) If no authorship is attributed, list the title of the article as the "author" in the footnote, and the magazine title as the "author" in the bibliography. Do not include page numbers for online articles.

2. Alan Dyer, "The End of the World ... Again," *SkyNews*, November/December 2012, 38.

3. "The Rise of the Yuan: Turning from Green to Red," *Economist*, October 20, 2012, 68.

4. Wendell Steavenson, "Two Revolutions: Women in the New Egypt," *The New Yorker*, November 12, 2012, http://www.newyorker.com/reporting/2012/11/12/121112fa_fact_steavenson.

Dyer, Alan. "The End of the World ... Again." *SkyNews*, November/December 2012, 38–39.

Economist. "The Rise of the Yuan: Turning from Green to Red." October 20, 2012, 67–68.

Steavenson, Wendell. "Two Revolutions: Women in the New Egypt." *The New Yorker*, November 12, 2012. http://www.newyorker.com/reporting/2012/11/12/121112fa_fact_steavenson.

16. **newspaper articles**: The basic principles to follow with newspaper articles or editorials are the same as with magazine articles (see above). Give page numbers in the note if your source is a hard copy rather than an electronic version, but indicate section designation alone in the Bibliography entry.

1. Konrad Yakabuski, "Many Looking for Meaning in Vice-Presidential Debate," *The Globe and Mail*, October 12, 2012, A3.

2. Claudia La Rocco, "Where Chekhov Meets Christopher Walken," *New York Times*, January 2, 2013, http://theater.nytimes.com/2013/01/03/theater/reviews/there-there-by-kristen-kosmas-at-the-chocolate-factory.html?ref=theater&_r=0.

La Rocco, Claudia. "Where Chekhov Meets Christopher Walken." *New York Times*, January 2, 2013, http://theater.nytimes.com/2013/01/03/theater/reviews/there-there-by-kristen-kosmas-at-the-chocolate-factory.html?ref=theater&_r=0.

Yakabuski, Konrad. "Many Looking for Meaning in Vice-Presidential Debate." *The Globe and Mail*, October 12, 2012, sec. A.

17. **journal articles:** The basic principles are the same as with magazine articles, but volume number, and issue number after *no.* (if the journal is published more than once a year), should be included as well as the date. Give page numbers where available. For online journal articles, provide the DOI, if available, rather than the URL.

1. Paul Barker, "The Impact of Class Size on the Classroom Behaviour of Special Needs Students: A Longitudinal Study," *Educational Quarterly* 25, no. 4 (2004): 88.

2. Maciel Santos and Ana Guedes, "The Profitability of Slave Labour and the 'Time' Effect," *African Economic History* 36 (2008): 23.

3. Thomas Hurka, "Virtuous Act, Virtuous Dispositions," *Analysis* 66, no. 1 (2006): 72.

4. Ruth Groenhout, "The 'Brain Drain' Problem: Migrating Medical Professionals and Global Health Care," *International Journal of Feminist Approaches to Bioethics* 5, no. 1 (2012): 17, doi: 10.2979/intjfemappbio.5.1.1.

Barker, Paul. "The Impact of Class Size on the Classroom Behaviour of Special Needs Students: A Longitudinal Study." *Educational Quarterly* 25, no. 4 (2004): 87–99.

Groenhout, Ruth. "The 'Brain Drain' Problem: Migrating Medical Professionals and Global Health Care." *International Journal of Feminist Approaches to Bioethics* 5, no. 1 (2012): 1–24, doi: 10.2979/intjfemappbio.5.1.1.

Hurka, Thomas. "Virtuous Act, Virtuous Dispositions." *Analysis* 66, no. 1 (2006): 69–76.

Santos, Maciel, and Ana Guedes. "The Profitability of Slave Labour and the 'Time' Effect." *African Economic History* 36 (2008): 1–26.

18. **films and video recordings**: Include the director's name, the city of production, the production company, and date. Add the medium of publication if the film is recorded on DVD or videocassette.

> 5. *Memento*, directed by Christopher Nolan (Universal City, CA: Summit Entertainment, 2000), DVD.
> 6. *Beasts of the Southern Wild*, directed by Behn Zeitlin (Los Angeles: Fox Searchlight Pictures, 2012).

> *Beasts of the Southern Wild*. Directed by Behn Zeitlin. Los Angeles: Fox Searchlight Pictures, 2012.
> *Memento*. Directed by Christopher Nolan. Universal City, CA: Summit Entertainment, 2000. DVD.

19. **television broadcasts**: Start with the title of the show; then give the episode number, broadcast date, and network. Include the names of the director and writer.

> 1. *Mad Men*, episodes no. 53–54, first broadcast March 25, 2012, by AMC, directed by Jennifer Getzinger and written by Matthew Weiner.

> *Mad Men*. Episodes no. 53–54, first broadcast March 25, 2012, by AMC. Directed by Jennifer Getzinger and written by Matthew Weiner.

20. **sound recordings**: Include the original date of recording if it is different from the recording release date, as well as the recording number and medium.

> 1. Glenn Gould, performance of *Goldberg Variations*, by Johann Sebastian Bach, recorded 1981, CBS MK 37779, 1982, compact disc.

Gould, Glenn. Performance of *Goldberg Variations*. By Johann Sebastian Bach. Recorded 1981. CBS MK 37779, 1982, compact disc.

21. **interviews and personal communications**: Notes and bibliography entries begin with the name of the person interviewed. Only interviews that are broadcast, published, or available online appear in the bibliography.

7. Louise Erdrich, interview by Bill Moyers, *Bill Moyers Journal*, PBS, April 9, 2010.

8. Ursula K. Le Guin, "Beyond Elvish," interview by Patrick Cox, *The World*, podcast audio, December 13, 2012, http://www.theworld.org/2012/12/beyond-elvish/.

9. Willie Nelson, "The Silver-Headed Stranger," interview by Andrew Goldman, *New York Times Magazine*, December 16, 2012, 12.

10. Herbert Rosengarten, telephone interview by author, January 17, 2013.

Erdrich, Louise. Interview by Bill Moyers. *Bill Moyers Journal*. PBS, April 9, 2010.

Le Guin, Ursula K. "Beyond Elvish." Interview by Patrick Cox. *The World*. Podcast audio. December 13, 2012. http://www.theworld.org/2012/12/beyond-elvish/.

Nelson, Willie. "The Silver-Headed Stranger." Interview by Andrew Goldman. *New York Times Magazine*, December, 2012, 12.

22. **book reviews**: The name of the reviewer (if it has been provided) should come first, as shown below:

1. Brian Leiter and Michael Weisberg, "Do You Only Have a Brain? On Thomas Nagel," review of *Why the Mate-*

rialist Neo-Darwinian Conception of Nature Is Almost Certainly False, by Thomas Nagel, *The Nation*, October 22, 2012, http://www.thenation.com/article/170334/do-you-only-have-brain-thomas-nagel.

Leiter, Brian, and Michael Weisberg. "Do You Only Have a Brain? On Thomas Nagel." Review of *Why the Materialist Neo-Darwinian Conception of Nature Is Almost Certainly False*, by Thomas Nagel. *The Nation*, October 22, 2012. http://www.thenation.com/article/170334/do-you-only-have-brain-thomas-nagel.

23. **blog posts:** Begin with the author's name, if there is one.

1. Karen Ho, "What Will Gioni's Biennale Look Like?," *The Art History Newsletter*, July 20, 2012, http://arthistorynewsletter.com/.

Ho, Karen. "What Will Gioni's Biennale Look Like?" *The Art History Newsletter*. July 20, 2012. http://arthistorynewsletter.com/.

24. **websites:** Unless the website title is also that of a book or periodical, do not put the site's title in italics. If possible, indicate when the site was last updated; otherwise, include your date of access.

1. The Camelot Project. University of Rochester, last modified December 21, 2012, http://www.lib.rochester.edu/camelot/cphome.stm.

The Camelot Project. University of Rochester. Last modified December 21, 2012. http://www.lib.rochester.edu/camelot/cphome.stm.

25. **online videos**: Include the author or principal performer, length of the video, and date of posting, if available, as well as the medium and its source.

> 1. Great Ape Trust, "Kanzi and Novel Sentences," YouTube video, 1:43, January 9, 2009, http://www.youtube.com/watch?v=2Dhc2zePJFE.

> Great Ape Trust. "Kanzi and Novel Sentences." YouTube video, 1:43. January 9, 2009. http://www.youtube.com/watch?v=2Dhc2zePJFE.

26. **tweets**: As of this book's press time, Chicago Style recommends that a tweet be described fully in the essay's text, as in the first example below. Following that is, as an alternative, Chicago Style's suggested format for a Twitter feed note citation. There is as yet no guidance for formatting a bibliography entry for a tweet, but one would not go far wrong in following Chicago Style's general guidelines for Web source entries; a suggested example is given in what follows.

> • Jack Welch (@jack_welch) quickly lost credibility when, on October 5, 2012 at 5:35 a.m., he tweeted that the U. S. Bureau of Labor had manipulated monthly unemployment rate statistics in order to boost the post-debate Obama campaign: "Unbelievable jobs numbers..these Chicago guys will do anything..can't debate so change numbers."[1]

> 1. Jack Welch, Twitter post, October 5, 2012, 5:35 a.m., http://twitter.com/jack_welch.

> Welch, Jack. Twitter post. October 5, 2012, 5:35 a.m. http://twitter.com/jack_welch.

O *Chicago Style Sample*

A sample of text with citations in Chicago style appears below. Note that a full sample essay in Chicago style appears on the adjunct website associated with this book.

Urban renewal is as much a matter of psychology as it is of bricks and mortar. As Paul Goldberger has described, there have been many plans to revitalize Havana.[1] But both that city and the community of Cuban exiles in Florida remain haunted by a sense of absence and separation. As Lourdes Casal reminds us,

> Exile
>
> is living where there is no house whatever in
>
> which we were ever children.[2]

The psychology of outsiders also makes a difference. Part of the reason Americans have not much noticed the dire plight of their fifth-largest city is that it does not "stir the national imagination."[3] Conversely, there has been far more concern over the state of cities

---

1   Paul Goldberger, "Annals of Preservation: Bringing Back Havana," *The New Republic*, January 2005, 54.

2   Lourdes Casal, "Definition," trans. Elizabeth Macklin, *The New Yorker*, January 26, 1998, 79.

3   Witold Rybczynski, "The Fifth City," review of *A Prayer for the City*, by Buzz Bissinger, *New York Review of Books*, February 5, 1998, 13.

such as New Orleans and Quebec, whose history and architecture excite the romantic imagination. As Nora Phelps has discussed,[4] the past is in itself a key trigger for romantic notions, and it is no doubt inevitable that cities whose history is particularly visible will engender passionate attachments. And as Stephanie Wright and Carole King have detailed in an important case study,[5] almost all French-speaking Quebecers feel their heritage to be bound up with that of Quebec City. (Richard Ford's character Frank Bascombe has suggested that "New Orleans defeats itself" by longing "for a mystery it doesn't have and never will, if it ever did,"[6] but this remains a minority view.)

Georgiana Gibson[7] is also among those who have investigated the interplay between urban psychology and urban reality. Gibson's personal website now includes the first of a set of working models she is developing in an attempt to represent the effects of psychological schemata on the landscape.

---

4   Nora Phelps, "Pastness and the Foundations of Romanticism," *Romanticism on the Net* 11 (May 2001): par. 14, http://users .ox.ac.uk/~scato385/phelpsmws.htm (accessed March 4, 2009).

5   Stephanie Wright and Carole King, *Quebec: A History*, 2 vols. (Montreal: McGill-Queen's University Press, 2003).

6   Richard Ford, *The Sportswriter*, 2nd ed. (New York: Random House, 1995), 48.

7   Georgiana Gibson, *Cities in the Twentieth Century* (Boston: Beacon, 2004).

The bibliography relating to the above text would be as follows:

Bibliography

Casal, Lourdes. "Definition." Translated by Elizabeth Macklin. *The New Yorker*, January 26, 1998, 79.

Ford, Richard. *The Sportswriter*. 2nd ed. New York: Random House, 1995.

Gibson, Georgiana. *Cities in the Twentieth Century*. Boston: Beacon, 2012.

---. Homepage. http:www.geography.by/u.edu/GIBSON/personal .htm (accessed March 4, 2013).

Goldberger, Paul. "Annals of Preservation: Bringing Back Havana." *The New Yorker*, January 26, 2005, 50–62. http://www .findarticles.com.goldberg.p65.jn.htm (accessed March 4, 2009).

Phelps, Nora. "Pastness and the Foundations of Romanticism." *Romanticism on the Net* 11 (May 2001). http://users.ox.ac .uk/~scato385/phelpsmws.htm (accessed March 4, 2009).

Rybczynski, Witold. "The Fifth City." Review of *A Prayer for the City*, by Buzz Bissinger. *New York Review of Books*, February 5, 1998, 12–14.

Wright, Stephanie, and Carole King. *Quebec: A History*. 2 vols. Montreal: McGill-Queen's University Press, 2012.

Among the details to notice in this reference system:

- Where two or more works by the same author are included in the bibliography, they are normally arranged alphabetically by title.

- All major words in titles and subtitles are capitalized.

- Date of publication must appear, where known. Provision of your date of access to electronic materials may be helpful, but is not required.

- Commas are used to separate elements within a footnote, and, in many circumstances, periods separate these same elements in the bibliographic entry.

- When a work has appeared in an edited collection, information on the editors must be included in the reference.

- First authors' first and last names are reversed in the bibliography.

- Translators must be noted both in footnotes and in the bibliography.

- Publisher as well as city of publication should be given.

- Months and publisher names are not abbreviated.

- The day of the month comes after the name of the month.

- Online references should *not* include the revision date but may include the date on which you visited the site (access date).

CSE Style

◎ CSE Style

The Council of Science Editors (CSE) style of documentation is commonly used in the natural sciences and the physical sciences. Guidelines are set out in *Scientific Style and Format: The CSE Manual for Authors, Editors, and Publishers*, 7th ed. (2006). The key features of CSE style are outlined below, and short sample essays using the three formats of the CSE documentation system follow at the end of this section.

In-text Citation: Citations in CSE style may follow three alternative formats: a **citation-name** format, a **citation-sequence** format, or a **name-year** format.

In the **citation-name** format, a reference list is compiled and arranged alphabetically by author. Each reference is then assigned a number in sequence, with the first alphabetical entry receiving the number 1, the second the number 2, and so on. Whenever you refer in your text to the reference labelled with number 3, for example, you use either a superscript number 3 (in one variation) or the same number in parentheses (in another).

- The difficulties first encountered in this experiment have been accounted for, according to Zelinsky[3]. However, the variables still have not been sufficiently well controlled for this type of experiment, argues Gibson[1].

- The difficulties first encountered in this experiment have been accounted for, according to Zelinsky (3). However, the variables still have not been sufficiently well controlled for this type of experiment, argues Gibson (1).

In the **citation-sequence** format, superscript numbers (or numbers in parentheses) are inserted after the mention of any source. The first source mentioned receives number 1, the second number 2, and so on.

- The difficulties first encountered in this experiment have been accounted for, according to Zelinsky[1]. However, the variables still have not been sufficiently well controlled for this type of experiment, argues Gibson[2].
- The difficulties first encountered in this experiment have been accounted for, according to Zelinsky (1). However, the variables still have not been sufficiently well controlled for this type of experiment, argues Gibson (2).

Reuse the number you first assign to a source whenever you refer to it again.

In the **name-year** format, you cite the author name and year of publication in parentheses:

- The key contributions to the study of variables in the 2000s (Gibson et al. 2008; Soames 2009; Zelinsky 2007) have been strongly challenged in recent years.

For two authors, list both, separated by *and* only; for more than two authors, give the first author's surname, followed by *et al.*

List of References: Citations in CSE style must correspond to items in a list of References.

In the **citation-name** format, entries are arranged alphabetically and assigned a number.

1. Gibson DL, Lampman GM, Kriz FR, Taylor DM. Introduction to statistical techniques in the sciences. 2nd ed. New York: MacQuarrie Learning; 2008. 1254 p.
2. Soames G. Variables in large database experiments. J Nat Hist. 2009; 82: 1811–41.
3. Zelinsky KL. The study of variables: an overview. New York: Academic; 2007. 216 p.

In the **citation-sequence** format, the references are listed in the sequence in which they have been cited in the text.

1. Zelinsky KL. The study of variables: an overview. New York: Academic; 2007. 216 p.
2. Gibson DL, Lampman GM, Kriz FR, Taylor DM. Introduction to statistical techniques in the sciences. 2nd ed. New York: MacQuarrie Learning; 2008. 1254 p.
3. Soames G. Variables in large database experiments. J Nat Hist. 2009; 82: 1811–41.

In the **name-year** format, the references are listed alphabetically, and the year of publication is given prominence.

Gibson DL, Lampman GM, Kriz FR, Taylor DM. 2008. Introduction to statistical techniques in the sciences. 2nd ed. New York: MacQuarrie Learning. 1254 p.

Soames G. 2009. Variables in large database experiments. J Nat Hist. 82: 1811–41.

Zelinsky KL. 2007. The study of variables: an overview. New York: Academic. 216 p.

The basic principles of the system are the same regardless of whether one is citing a book, an article in a journal or magazine, a newspaper article, or an electronic document. Here are the main details.

Author names in the References list are all inverted, with initials given instead of full first names. Initials have no periods after them, and no commas separate them from surnames. If a source in the References list has two to ten authors, include all of them; do not include *and* at any point in the list. For more than ten authors, give the names of the first ten, with *and others* following the last one listed.

Capitalize all major words in the titles of periodicals (journals, magazines, and newspapers). For books and articles, capitalize only the first words of the title, as well as any proper nouns. Abbreviate journal titles according to standardized guidelines. You can find the accepted abbreviation of a journal title at the Genamics JournalSeek site online (http://journalseek.net/); enter the journal's full title into the *Search Title* field.

Entries for books include the city of publication, the publisher, and the date of publication.

Entries for periodical articles should include the date: for journal articles, give the year; for magazine articles, give the year and month (abbreviated); for newspaper articles, give the year, the month (abbreviated), and the day.

For online sources, include all of the publication information that you would for print sources. Add *[Internet]* after the book or periodical title. The position of the date of access (e.g., *cited 2013 Feb 13*) varies according to which format you use. Give the URL after *Available from:*, and then, if there is one, the DOI (digital object identifier—a string of numbers, letters, and punctuation, beginning with *10*, usually located on the first or copyright page). Do not put a period at the end of a DOI or a URL (unless it ends with a slash).

O *CSE Style Sample*

The following is written using the citation-sequence format.

Over the centuries scientific study has evolved into several distinct disciplines. Physics, chemistry, and biology were established early on; in the nineteenth and twentieth centuries they were joined by others, such as geology and ecology. Much as the disciplines have their separate spheres, the sphere of each overlaps those of others. This may be most obvious in the case of ecology, which some have claimed to be a discipline that makes a holistic approach to science respectable[1]. In the case of geology, as soon as it became clear in the nineteenth century that the fossil record of geological life would be central to the future of geology, the importance of connecting with the work of biologists became recognized[2]. Nowadays it is not surprising to have geological research conducted jointly by biologists and geologists (e.g., the work of Newton, Trewman, and Elser[3]). And, with the acceptance of "continental drift" theories in the 1960s and 1970s, physics came to be increasingly relied on for input into discussions of such topics as collision tectonics (e.g., Pfiffton, Earn, and Brome[4]).

The growth of the subdiscipline of biochemistry at the point of overlap between biology and chemistry is well known, but many are unaware that the scope of biological physics is almost as broad; Frauenfrommer[5] provides a helpful survey. Today it is

CSE Style

not uncommon, indeed, to see research such as the recent study by Corel, Marks, and Hutner[6], or that by Balmberg, Passano, and Proule[7], both of which draw on biology, chemistry, and physics simultaneously.

Interdisciplinary scientific exploration has also been spurred by the growth of connections between the pure sciences and applied sciences such as meteorology, as even a glance in the direction of recent research into such topics as precipitation[8] or cratonising[9] confirms. But to the extent that science is driven by the applied, will it inextricably become more and more driven by commercial concerns? Christopher Haupt-Lehmann[10] thinks not.

The citations above would connect to References as follows:

References

1. Branmer A. Ecology in the twentieth century: a history. New Haven: Yale UP; 2004. 320 p.

2. Lyell C. Principles of geology. London: John Murray; 1830. 588 p.

3. Newton MJ, Trewman NH, Elser S. A new jawless invertebrate from the Middle Devonian. Paleontology [Internet]. 2011 [cited 2013 Mar 5]; 44(1): 43–52. Available from: http://www.onlinejournals.paleontology.44/html doi:10.1136/p.330.6500.442

4. Pfiffton QA, Earn PK, Brome C. Collision tectonics and dynamic modelling. Tectonics 2012; 19(6): 1065–94.

5. Frauenfrommer H. Introduction. In: Frauenfrommer H, Hum G, Glazer RG, editors. Biological physics third international symposium; 1998 Mar 8–9; Santa Fe, NM [Melville, NY]: American Institute of Physics. 386 p.

6. Corel B, Marks VJ, Hutner H. The modelling effect of Elpasolites. Chem Sci 2013; 55(10): 935–38.

7. Balmberg NJ, Passano C, Proule AB. The Lorenz-Fermi-Pasta-Ulam experiment. Physica D [Internet]. 2005 [cited 2013 Mar 7]; 138(1): 1–47. Available from: http://www.elseviere.com/locate/phys

8. Caine JS, Gross SM, Baldwin G. Melting effect as a factor in precipitation-type forecasting. Weather Forecast 2010; 15(6): 700–14.

9. Pendleton AJ. Gawler craton. Reg Geo 2001; 11: 999–1016.

10. Haupt-Lehmann C. Money and science: the latest word. New York Times 2001 Mar 23; Sect. D:22 (col 1).

Among the details to notice in the citation-sequence format of the CSE style:

- The entries in References are listed in the order they first appear in the text.

- Unpunctuated initials rather than first names are used in References.

- The date appears near the end of the reference, before any page reference.

- Only the first words of titles are capitalized (except for proper nouns and the abbreviated titles of journals).

- When a work has appeared in an edited collection the names of the editor(s) as well as the author(s) must appear in the reference.

- Publisher as well as city of publication should be given.

- Months and journal names are generally abbreviated.

- References to electronic publications include the date of access as well as date of publication or latest revision.

- Names of articles appear with no surrounding quotation marks; names of books and journal titles appear with no italics.

Here is the same passage with the CSE name-year format used:

Over the centuries scientific study has evolved into several distinct disciplines. Physics, chemistry, and biology were established early on; in the nineteenth and twentieth centuries, they were joined by others, such as geology and ecology. Much as the disciplines have their separate spheres, the sphere of each overlaps those of others. This may be most obvious in the case of ecology, which some have claimed to be a discipline that makes a holistic approach to science respectable (Branmer 2004). In the case of geology, as soon as it became clear in the nineteenth century that the fossil record of geological life would be central to the future of geology, the importance of connecting with the work of biologists became recognized (Lyell 1830). Nowadays it is not surprising to have geological research conducted jointly by biologists and geologists (e.g., Newton, Trewman, and Elser 2011). And, with the acceptance of "continental drift" theories in the 1960s and 1970s, physics came to be increasingly relied on for input into discussions of such topics as collision tectonics (e.g., Pfiffton, Earn, and Brome 2012).

The growth of the subdiscipline of biochemistry at the point of overlap between biology and chemistry is well known, but many are unaware that the scope of biological physics is almost as broad; Frauenfrommer (1998) provides a helpful survey. Today it is not uncommon, indeed, to see research such as the recent study by Corel, Marks, and Hutner (2013) or that by Balmberg, Passano, and Proule (2005), both of which draw on biology, chemistry, and physics simultaneously.

Interdisciplinary scientific exploration has also been spurred by the growth of connections between the pure sciences and applied sciences such as meteorology, as even a glance in the direction of recent research into such topics as precipitation (Caine, Gross, and Baldwin 2010) or cratonising (Pendleton 2001) confirms. But to the extent that science is driven by the applied, will it inextricably become more and more driven by commercial concerns? Christopher Haupt-Lehmann (2001) thinks not.

The citations above would connect to References as follows:

References

Balmberg NJ, Passano C, Proule AB. 2005. The Lorenz-Fermi-Pasta-Ulam experiment. Physica D [Internet] [cited 2013 Mar 7]; 138(1): 1–47. Available from: http://www.elseviere.com/locate/phys

Branmer A. 2004. Ecology in the twentieth century: a history. New Haven: Yale UP. 320 p.

Caine JS, Gross SM, Baldwin G. 2010. Melting effect as a factor in precipitation-type forecasting. Weather Forecast. 15(6): 700–14.

Corel B, Marks VJ, Hutner H. 2013. The modelling effect of Elpasolites. Chem Sci. 55(10): 935–38.

Frauenfrommer H. 1998. Introduction. In Frauenfrommer H, Hum G, Glazer RG, editors. Mar 8–9. Biological physics third international symposium. Santa Fe, NM [Melville, NY]: American Institute of Physics. 386 p.

Haupt-Lehmann C. 2001 Mar 23. Money and science: the latest word. New York Times; Sect D:22 (col 1).

Lyell C. 1830. Principles of geology. London: John Murray. 588 p.

Newton MJ, Trewman NH, Elser S. 2011. A new jawless invertebrate from the Middle Devonian. Paleontology [Internet] [cited 2013 Mar 5]; 44(1): 43–52. Available from: http://www.onlinejournals.paleontology.44/html doi:10.1136/p.330.6500.442

Pendleton AJ. 2001. Gawler craton. Reg Geol; 11: 999–1016.

Pfiffton QA, Earn PK, Brome C. 2012. Collision tectonics and dynamic modelling. Tectonics. 19(6): 1065–94.

Among the details to notice in the name-year reference system:

- The entries in References are listed in alphabetical order by author.

- Unpunctuated initials rather than first names are used in References.

- The date appears immediately after the author name(s) at the beginning of the reference.

- The in-text citation comes before the period or comma in the surrounding sentence.

- Only the first words of titles are capitalized (except for proper nouns and the abbreviated titles of journals).

- When a work has appeared in an edited collection the names of the editor(s) as well as the author(s) must appear in the reference.

- The word *and* is used for in-text citations of works with more than one author—but not in the corresponding reference list entry.

- Publisher as well as city of publication should be given.

- Months and journal names are generally abbreviated.

- References to electronic publications include the date of access as well as the date of publication or latest revision.

- Names of articles appear with no surrounding quotation marks; names of books, journals, etc. appear with no italics.

Here is the same passage again, this time using the CSE citation-name format:

Over the centuries scientific study has evolved into several distinct disciplines. Physics, chemistry, and biology were established early on; in the nineteenth and twentieth centuries they were joined by others, such as geology and ecology. Much as the disciplines have their separate spheres, the sphere of each overlaps those of others. This may be most obvious in the case of ecology, which some have claimed to be a discipline that makes a holistic approach to science respectable[2]. In the case of geology, as soon as it became clear in the nineteenth century that the fossil record of geological life would be central to the future of geology, the importance of connecting with the work of biologists became recognized[7]. Nowadays it is not surprising to have geological research conducted jointly by biologists and geologists (e.g., Newton, Trewman, and Elser[8]). And, with the acceptance of "continental drift" theories in the 1960s and 1970s, physics came to be increasingly relied on for input into discussions of such topics as collision tectonics (e.g., Pfiffton, Earn, and Brome[10]).

The growth of the subdiscipline of biochemistry at the point of overlap between biology and chemistry is well known, but many are unaware that the scope of biological physics is almost as broad; Frauenfrommer[5] provides a helpful survey. Today it is not uncommon, indeed, to see research such as the recent study by Corel, Marks, and Hutner[4] or that by Balmberg, Passano, and Proule[1], both of which draw on biology, chemistry, and physics simultaneously.

Interdisciplinary scientific exploration has also been spurred by the growth of connections between the pure sciences and applied sciences such as meteorology, as even a glance in the direction of recent research into such topics as precipitation[3] or cratonising[9] confirms. But to the extent that science is driven by the applied, will it inextricably become more and more driven by commercial concerns? Christopher Haupt-Lehmann[6] thinks not.

CSE Style

The citations above would connect to References as follows:

References

1. Balmberg NJ, Passano C, Proule AB. The Lorenz-Fermi-Pasta-Ulam experiment. Physica D [Internet]. 2005 [cited 2013 Mar 7]; 138(1): 1–47. Available from: http://www.elseviere.com/locate/phys

2. Branmer A. Ecology in the twentieth century: a history. New Haven: Yale UP; 2004. 320 p.

3. Caine, JS, Gross SM, Baldwin G. Melting effect as a factor in precipitation-type forecasting. Weather Forecast 2010; 15(6): 700–14.

4. Corel B, Marks VJ, Hutner H. The modelling effect of Elpasolites. Chem Sci 2013; 55(10): 935–38.

5. Frauenfrommer H. Introduction. Frauenfrommer H, Hum G, Glazer RG, editors. Biological physics third international symposium; 1998 Mar 8–9; Santa Fe, NM [Melville, NY]: American Institute of Physics. 386 p.

6. Haupt-Lehmann C. Money and science: the latest word. New York Times 2001 Mar 23; Sect. D:22 (col 1).

7. Lyell C. Principles of geology. London: John Murray; 1830. 588 p.

8. Newton MJ, Trewman NH, Elser S. A new jawless invertebrate from the Middle Devonian. Paleontology [Internet]. 2011 [cited 2013 Mar 5]; 44(1): 43–52. Available from: http://www.onlinejournals.paleontology.44/html doi:10.1136/p.330.6500.442

9. Pendleton AJ. Gawler craton. Reg Geo 2001; 11: 999–1016.

10. Pfiffton QA, Earn PK, Brome C. Collision tectonics and dynamic modelling. Tectonics 2012; 19(6): 1065–94.

Among the details to notice in the citation-name format of the CSE style:

- The entries in References are numbered and listed in alphabetical order according to author.

- Unpunctuated initials rather than first names are used in References.

- The date appears near the end of the reference, before any page reference.

- Only the first words of titles are capitalized (except for proper nouns and the abbreviated titles of journals).

- When a work has appeared in an edited collection the names of the editor(s) as well as the author(s) must appear in the reference.

- The word *and* is used for in-text citations of works with more than one author—but not in the corresponding reference.

- Publisher as well as city of publication should be given.

- Months and journal names are generally abbreviated.

- References to electronic publications include the date of access as well as date of publication or latest revision.

- Names of articles appear with no surrounding quotation marks; names of books and journal titles appear with no italics.

◎ Sample Essay (MLA Style)

cover page (may not be required by some instructors)

What Limits to Freedom?

Freedom of Expression and the Brooklyn Museum's

"Sensation" Exhibit

all text centred

by Melissa Davis

Prof. K. D. Smith

Humanities 205

16 June 2015

Melissa Davis

Davis 1

Professor Smith

Humanities 205

16 June 2015

What Limits to Freedom?

Freedom of Expression and the Brooklyn Museum's

"Sensation" Exhibit

       For over a century public galleries in Western democracies have

been forums not only for displaying works by "old Masters" but also

for presenting art that is new, as well as ideas that are sometimes

radical and controversial. In the United States that tradition has

been under wide attack in the past generation. Various political and

religious leaders have criticized exhibits of works of art that they claim

offend against notions of public decency, and have crusaded against

providing public funding for the creation or display of such works.

The largest such controversy of the past generation was sparked by

the display of a painting entitled "The Holy Virgin Mary," by the

British artist Chris Ofili at the Brooklyn Museum in 1999. Though

the image appears inoffensive at a distance, the artist has affixed

to the painting cutouts of body parts from magazines, and has

incorporated clumps of elephant dung into the piece, both below

the main body of the work as if supporting it and as part of the

Davis 2

collage. The uproar that surrounded the painting's exhibition led both to a widely publicized court case and to an ongoing campaign to support "decency" in artistic expression. Should such art be banned? Should it be exhibited at public expense? In the course of the Ofili controversy cultural conservatives raised legitimate concerns about the obligation of any society to provide funding for activities of which it disapproves. This essay will argue, however, that the greater concern is in the other direction; a free society must continue to provide opportunities for the free expression both of artistic vision and of controversial thought.

The Ofili piece was part of a much-hyped exhibit entitled "Sensation: Young British Artists from the Saatchi Collection." As the title indicated, the show was made up entirely of works from one collection, that of the wealthy British advertising executive Charles Saatchi.[1] The exhibition had been shown first at the Royal Academy of Arts in London and then at a major gallery in Berlin. (In London what sparked controversy was not Ofili's work but rather a realistic painting by Marcus Harvey of child-murderer Myra Hindley that incorporated hundreds of children's handprints into the image.) Bringing the show to Brooklyn cost one million dollars—a cost covered in part by Christie's, a London auctioneer—and from the outset it could be argued that the museum was courting controversy.

first paragraph ends with a statement of the essay's thesis

MLA Sample Essay

numbered note for additional information provided as an aside

Davis 3

It claimed in its advertising that the exhibition "may cause shock, vomiting, confusion, panic, euphoria, and anxiety. If you suffer from high blood pressure, a nervous disorder, or palpitations, you should consult your doctor" (qtd. in Barry and Vogel).

parenthetical reference; Internet source has no page number

No doubt that warning was tongue-in-cheek, but there was nothing ironic about the angry reactions provoked by the show in general and directed toward the Ofili piece in particular. On one side art critics and civil libertarians were full of praise; in *The New York Times* the work was praised as "colourful and glowing" (Kimmelman). On the other side John Cardinal O'Connor called it "an attack on religion," and the president of the Catholic League for Religious and Civil Rights called on citizens to picket the exhibition (Vogel). The United States Senate and the House of Representatives both passed resolutions condemning the exhibit. Even more vehement was the response of New York Mayor Rudy Giuliani; he declared himself "offended" and the work itself "disgusting" (Barry and Vogel). As Peter Cramer has detailed, Giuliani's comments received widespread attention in the press—especially the informal remark "I mean, this is like, sick stuff," from which the phrase "sick stuff" was extracted for repeated circulation. But Giuliani and Deputy Mayor Joseph J. Lhota, the city administration's "enforcer in the case" (Barbaro 2), did much more than comment. They ordered that ongoing city funding

parenthetical references at end of short quotations followed by punctuation

MLA Sample Essay

of the museum be withheld until the offensive work was removed, and launched eviction proceedings against the museum. Other conservative politicians—then-Texas Governor George W. Bush prominent among them—spoke out in support of Giuliani's stand ("Bush Backs Giuliani").

What was the substance of Mayor Giuliani's case? Here is how he explained his stance to the press:

> You don't have a right to a government subsidy to desecrate someone else's religion. And therefore we will do everything that we can to remove funding from the [museum] until the director comes to his senses and realizes that if you are a government subsidized enterprise then you can't do things that desecrate the most personal and deeply held views of people in society.
> (Brooklyn Institute of Arts and Sciences v. City of New York 7)

In Giuliani's view, the constitution's guarantee of freedom of speech was not the central issue:

> "If somebody wants to do that privately and pay for that privately . . . that's what the First Amendment is all about," he said. "You can be offended by it and upset by it, and you don't have to go see it, if somebody else is paying for it. But to have the government subsidize something like that is outrageous."
> (qtd. in Vogel)

long quotations indented— no quotation marks used except for quotation within a quotation

The issue for Guiliani, then, is not one of censorship per se. He is not arguing that works of art should be banned for causing offense to a significant segment of the public; it is merely the provision of any government funding for such activity that he finds "outrageous."

But is it in fact outrageous? Let us examine the implications of Giuliani's argument. According to him, government should never provide funding for activities that some people may find deeply offensive. But governments have long funded much artistic and intellectual activity in advance on the grounds that such activity in general represents a social good, without knowing precisely what sort of artistic work will be created or exhibited, what results academic research may come up with, and so on. If such funding were to be always contingent on no one ever being deeply offended by the results of the artistic or intellectual activity, the effect would be to severely damage freedom of speech and expression. (Here it is important to note that the actions Giuliani took were retroactive; the annual funding for the museum had not been provided with strings attached.[2])

Social conservatives are often characterized as favouring censorship of any material they find offensive; to be fair, that is clearly not the position Giuliani takes here. Nor is the issue whether or not the material is offensive; Hillary Clinton, for example, agreed that works such as that by Ofili were "objectionable" and "offensive" (qtd. in Nagourney), while opposing any punitive actions against the museum. Rather, the issue at stake is under what conditions government has an obligation to fund controversial artistic or intellectual activity. At issue here are both a quite narrow and specific question, and a much broader one. The narrow question is this: to what degree must public officials be held to prior commitments of the sort that were involved in this case?

To this question at least, it does not seem difficult to find an answer: a continuing obligation surely does indeed exist where a prior commitment has been made. As Judge Nina Gershon put it in her eventual ruling on the case,

> the issue is . . . whether the museum, having been allocated a general operating subsidy, can now be penalized with the loss of that subsidy, and ejectment from a City-owned building, because of the perceived viewpoint of the works in that exhibit. The answer to that question is no. (Brooklyn Institute v. City of New York 17)

Where such a commitment has been made, it can only be fairly broken if the activity has in some way contravened previously agreed-on guidelines or if it has broken the law. If, for example, a work of art or of literature is thought to violate laws against obscenity, laws concerning hate crimes, laws concerning libel and slander—or, indeed, laws concerning cruelty to animals, as in the cases of certain "works of art" in recent years[3]—then legal recourse is available. But not even the most vociferous of the opponents of the "Sensation" exhibit suggested that Ofili, the curators, or anyone else had broken the law. Moreover, the ongoing funding for the Museum had never been made contingent on the institution's exhibits never offending anyone. There were therefore no just grounds for taking punitive action as Giuliani did.

But how much further than this should the obligation of government to fund controversial artistic or intellectual activity extend? Here we come to the broader issue: do governments have a general obligation to support and to fund such activity? The tradition of government support for artistic and intellectual activity in Western democracies has for many generations been one in which support was provided at "arm's length" from the political process; if judgements based on the merit of individual works need be made, they are typically made by bodies independent of government. That approach has stemmed from a number of sensible general principles. One such principle has been a recognition of the inherent value of intellectual and artistic activity. Another has been a recognition that such activity will sometimes be challenging, disturbing, even offensive

MLA Sample Essay

no citation needed for information that is common knowledge

or disgusting.[4] And a third has been that if politicians are involved in judging individual artistic or intellectual works, the judgements will tend to be made more on political and religious grounds than on intellectual and aesthetic ones. We value a society in which a wide range of free expression is supported, and we have come to expect that governments will provide a good deal of that support.

Despite the general support for these principles that exists in our society, we should not assume an unlimited obligation on the part of government. In particular, liberals and civil libertarians are unwise if they suggest that the obligation of the government to support artistic or intellectual endeavour is always a strong and compelling one, or that any failure of a government to provide financial support for such endeavour somehow constitutes censorship.[5] There is no clear agreement as to what constitutes art; it follows that there can be no legal or moral obligation to fund everything that may be classified as art. And to decide in advance not to subsidize an activity is not the same as censoring that activity; civil libertarians do not advance their case by equating the two. Indeed, as philosopher Peter Levine has pointed out, attempts to remove all restrictions on government support can easily backfire, since the law

> cannot compel governments to subsidize art in the first place. When the Supreme Court ruled in 1998 that individual artists

sentence structured so that it flows grammatically into quotation

MLA Sample Essay

may not be denied federal grants because of the content of
their work, Congress simply cancelled all support for individual
artists. (20)

It is never wise, then, for the artistic and intellectual communities to
press too hard for unrestricted government support.

It is perhaps an even greater mistake, however, for cultural
conservatives to seek to restrict government support to work that
conforms to their definition of "decency." The moral obligation of
government to support a broad range of artistic and intellectual
expression may be a relatively weak one, but if we cast it aside we are
choosing to narrow ourselves, to discourage rather than encourage the
sorts of challenge from new ideas and new artistic expressions that
continually replenish the red blood cells of democratic society.

In approaching such questions we should ask ourselves what
really constitutes freedom of thought, speech, and expression. One
defining pillar is legal: constitutional guarantees of freedom and the
case law that has helped to define them.[6] But is that all there is to it?
A moment's reflection should make it clear that a great deal else is
involved. Regardless of what is allowed or prohibited, if there exists
a scarcity of art galleries—or of book publishers, or of academic
journals, or of newspapers, or of radio and television stations—that
are willing to put forward original and controversial works of art,

or works of scholarly research, or political treatises, then freedom of speech and expression is *in practice* severely limited.[7] And economic reality dictates that a number of valued activities, including academic research as well as many of the arts, would be severely curtailed without some degree of public funding. If we choose as a society not to fund such activities we will inevitably be erecting real barriers against freedom of speech and expression, even if we have passed no laws restricting such freedoms. That is the reality at the heart of the "Sensation" controversy.

It is interesting that in the midst of the controversy Ofili's work itself became oddly invisible, lost in the clamour of arguments from principle on both sides of the debate. Photographic representations of "Holy Virgin Mary" are widely available on the Web,[8] and viewers coming to these after sampling the heat of the arguments surrounding the piece are likely to be surprised by how calm and pleasant an image is presented to them. Ofili himself was the recipient of the prestigious Turner Prize in 1998 and was already becoming widely recognized as one of the most important of his generation of British artists. Fairly typical are the comments of a writer in *Art in America*, one of the most authoritative journals of contemporary art criticism: "his paintings are a joy to behold. . . . His technique, as it becomes ever richer and more complex, is developing an emotional range to match

page number follows author's name in parenthetical reference

its decorative facility" (MacRitchie, 97). The painter, who was born in Britain to parents of Nigerian background, was raised a church-going Catholic—and remained so at the time he painted the controversial work. (Clearly critics' claims that "The Holy Virgin Mary" is offensive to Catholics cannot be true of all Catholics!)

Ofili has spoken interestingly of how in his art of that period he drew connections between the subjects of his work and the materials he used, including shiny varnish to make it seem that the subject of a painting is "in some ways more imagined than real" (Vogel), and, of course, the notorious balls of elephant dung that adorn the work and on which it rests.[9] Significantly, during that stage of his career Ofili incorporated dung into many of his works, including those portraying slaves and other African subjects. As Arthur C. Danto has pointed out, "since it is unlikely that as a black Anglo-African Ofili would have used dung to besmirch the slaves [in the picture "Afrobluff"], there is no reason to suppose he was bent on besmirching the Holy

MLA Sample Essay

quotation with author named in signal phrase; page number in parentheses

Virgin through its presence there either" (2). From one angle, Ofili clearly saw the use of dung as a way of connecting his paintings to his African heritage and of giving the paintings "a feeling that they've come from the earth" (Vogel). But his art of that period was also drawing connections between the superficially appealing nature of his images and the inherent unpleasantness of some of the materials he has used to create them:

> "The paintings themselves are very delicate abstractions, and
> I wanted to bring their beauty and decorativeness together
> with the ugliness of shit[10] and make them exist in a twilight
> zone—you know they're together, but you can't really ever feel
> comfortable about it." (qtd. in "Sensation")

Ofili's intention, in short, was to create a disturbing tension in the
mind of the viewer.

title cited
when work
has no
attributed
author

One does not need to endorse all of Ofili's theorizing about what
he does, or agree fully with the favourable assessments of the critics
in order to conclude that it would be unreasonable not to classify his
work as art. Even the narrowest and most conservative definitions
of art allow the term to be applied to work that many people find
pleasing to the eye and that many agree demonstrates creative skill.
Ofili's work unquestionably fulfills those criteria. More than that,
there is evidently a good deal of subtlety and nuance to both the
work and the ideas of this painter, far more than the polarized debate
swirling around the painting might suggest. Even if some find this art
offensive, it is hard not to think that on its merits Ofili's work deserves
to be widely exhibited.

In a narrow sense the controversy of the Ofili work and the
"Sensation" exhibit ended with a clear victory for the Brooklyn

MLA Sample Essay

Museum. Federal Judge Nina Gershon ruled that in these circumstances the City of New York's attempt to shut down the exhibit constituted a violation of the First Amendment—the Constitutional guarantee of freedom of expression—and in March of 2000 the City and the museum reached an agreement under the terms of which all further lawsuits were dropped and the City agreed to contribute 5.8 million dollars towards a museum restoration project. (The museum re-opened in 2004 after the completion of restorations.)

In a wider sense, however, the outcome is far less certain. In 2001 Mayor Giuliani attempted to develop "decency standards" intended to restrict these sorts of works from being shown in future in publicly funded exhibitions, and such initiatives received strong support from the administration of George W. Bush. Among certain commentators the crusade against Ofili continued unabated long after the exhibit itself had ended. Phyllis Schlafly is one such crusader (2004); Tammy Bruce is another. In her best-selling book *The Death of Right and Wrong*, for example, Bruce used the case as an example in urging us to "make no mistake: the degrading of symbols important to Christianity is . . . propaganda meant to change your view of Christianity as a whole" (52).

Given the virulence of attacks of this sort, it would have been extraordinary had major museums and galleries not begun to back

italics used for titles of books, newspapers, journals, etc.

MLA Sample Essay

away from mounting exhibitions of work that they considered likely
to be controversial. Tellingly, the "Sensation" exhibit was never
seen after it closed in Brooklyn; the National Gallery of Australia
cancelled its plans to show the exhibit, and a Tokyo museum that had
expressed interest in exhibiting it thereafter did not in the end make
any commitment (Rosenbaum 41). In 2008, the San Francisco Art
Institute closed Adel Abdessemed's controversial "Don't Trust Me"
show after only a few days "for safety reasons" (DeBare B1) in the face
of protests by animals' rights groups and some artists, though there
had been no suggestion that any law had been broken, and though
condemnation of the show had been far from universal.[11]

Since 2008 controversies of this sort have been less common
in North America at public galleries and museums.[12] In the United
States, at least, that may have to do in part with a change in tone from
the federal government under the Obama administration. No doubt
in part it may also have to do with changes in tone in the world of
contemporary art; the urge to shock seems less widespread among
artists now than it was in the last decades of the twentieth century.
But it may well be that public galleries in North America have become
reluctant to risk being attacked in the way the Brooklyn Museum was
attacked over "Sensation."[13] It is striking that the most controversial
exhibit in any public gallery in recent years was not in any of the

MLA Sample Essay

great museums and galleries of the western democracies that have
long prided themselves on their openness. It was the historically staid
Hermitage Museum in St Petersburg, Russia, that risked the wrath
of the socially conservative citizenry by mounting the Chapman
brothers' "End of Fun" exhibition in 2012.[14]

In theory at least, public institutions in the United States,
Canada and Britain—universities and colleges[15] as well as museums
and galleries—have far more legal room than do those in partially free
countries such as Russia to risk controversy. But freedom of expression
is never only a matter of what is or is not legal. The preservation of
a truly open society requires, on the part of those who wish to allow
and to encourage freedom of expression, a moral determination that
is at least as strong as the moral determination of those who wish to
roll back its frontiers. Much as constitutional guarantees of freedom of
expression are important, even more so is whether we wish as a society
to narrow the range of what citizens may readily see or hear, or instead
to encourage the wide dissemination of information, opinion, and
artistic expression—even opinions and artistic expressions that some
may find offensive. In the years following the September 11, 2001
attack, it was understandable that many both within the United States
and around the world were prepared to accept some extraordinary new
restrictions on freedom—and many, of course, argue that the need for

MLA Sample Essay

such restrictions remains. But whatever security justifications there may be for such restrictions do not extend to the sphere of intellectual and artistic activity. If we wish to retain a robustly democratic society we should continue to choose the path of openness.

final
paragraph
restates
and
broadens
the essay's
main
argument

MLA Sample Essay

Notes

notes numbered as in text

1. Saatchi contributed $100,000 to mounting the show, the economics of which became another subject for controversy when it was shown in Brooklyn. As well as complaining about the content of the works in the exhibit, Mayor Rudy Giuliani and others suggested that the show had been intended in large part to raise the value of works in the Saatchi collection, and on those grounds, too, argued

each note indented

that the exhibit should not be receiving a subsidy from taxpayers.

2. Because its content was recognized as controversial, city officials had been provided in advance of the "Sensation" show with photographs and full descriptions of all pieces to be included in the exhibit, including the information that Ofili's works incorporated elephant dung into the images they portrayed. The mayor insisted that he personally had not been alerted to the content of the show beforehand, however.

3. Animal rights activists have protested against works by the renowned British artist Damien Hirst, which present, among other things, a sectioned cow and a bisected pig in formaldehyde cases. (Several such works by Hirst were included in the "Sensation" show.) In Toronto, art student Jesse Power and two friends pleaded guilty in 2001 to charges of animal cruelty and public mischief after making

MLA Sample Essay

what they called an art video recording their torturing and killing a
cat; the case again aroused controversy in 2004 following the release of
a documentary film about the incident, *Casuistry: The Art of Killing a
Cat*, directed by Noah Cowan and Piers Handling. See also the articles
by Christie Blatchford and by Gayle MacDonald, Note 11 below on
the 2008 "Don't Trust Me" exhibition in San Francisco, and Note 15
below on the 2013 ACAD controversy in Calgary.

4. There are many defenses of the principle that an open society
must make a place even for controversial or disgusting material. The case
for the other side is put by John Kekes in *A Case for Conservatism*; he
argues for what he terms "the moral importance of disgust" (100–109).

5. To be fair, although some individuals make assertions as
extreme as this one, responsible civil liberties organizations such as the
ACLU stop short of any such all-embracing claim.

6. The First Amendment to the American Constitution specifies
that Congress "shall make no law . . . abridging the freedom of
speech, or of the press; or the right of the people to assemble. . . ."
In American legal practice it has long been established that "freedom
of speech" should also cover other forms of expression—such as
artistic works. Other, more recent constitutions tend to make such
protections explicit; the Charter of Rights and Freedoms that forms
a central part of the Canadian Constitution, for example, protects

"freedom of thought, belief, opinion, and expression, including freedom of the press and other media of communication."

7. A good example of how such freedoms may be constrained is the March 2003 case in which Natalie Maines of the Dixie Chicks criticized George W. Bush—and promptly found that two media conglomerates controlling over 1,300 radio stations refused to play Dixie Chicks music. That case is discussed by Robert B. Reich in *Reason: Why Liberals Will Win the Battle for America.*

8. Among the many Web addresses at which photographs of the work may be found are www.artsjournal.com/issues/Brooklyn.htm and www.postmedia.net/999/ofili.htm and www.brooklynmuseum.org/opencollection/exhibitions/683.

9. Many who have attacked the piece have chosen to describe the dung as being "*smeared* on a Christian icon" (Bruce 39, my italics), which is substantially to misrepresent the nature of the work.

10. It is interesting to contemplate the impact diction may have on arguments such as this; it is difficult not to respond slightly differently depending on whether the material is referred to using the noun Ofili uses here or referred to less provocatively as "dung."

11. The show included video clips of the killing of animals in rural Mexico. The artist had evidently not arranged for the killings; he was merely recording local practice. For more on this and other

recent controversies, see the articles by Kenneth Baker and Phoebe Hoban.

12. Such controversies have been more common at private galleries, which do not run the risk of losing public funding, and which may even gain desired publicity from them. Notable private gallery controversies have occurred, for example, in 2010, when a protestor attacked a work associating Christianity with cannibalism at the Loveland Museum/Gallery in Colorado; and in 2012, when the Catholic League deplored the showing of Andress Serrano's 1980s work "Piss Christ" at a private gallery in New York.

13. It is noteworthy that, when Ofili's "The Holy Virgin Mary" was again exhibited in the New York area in 2014–15, it was at the New Museum—a privately owned gallery, not a public institution. The exhibition was greeted by rave reviews (see Smith and Tomkins), and little or no controversy. Perhaps in large part because Ofili's reputation as an artist of the first rank has continued to grow, "The Holy Virgin Mary" no longer seems to elicit such a vitriolic response. That much, at least, has changed over time. What has not changed since the close of the "Sensation" exhibit, though, is the reluctance of North American public institutions to mount shows that court controversy. In fact, the painting has been exhibited only once in a major public institution since the "Sensation" controversy—as part

MLA Sample Essay

of an Ofili retrospective at the Tate Modern in London in 2010. (The painting now belongs to David Walsh, owner of a private gallery in Hobart, Australia, where it is frequently on display.)

14. Among the objects included in the exhibition were a crucified image of Ronald McDonald and human figures forming swastika shapes. Hundreds of complaints regarding alleged blasphemy were made to the authorities. Legally, the issue was whether the exhibit violated a law against the incitement of hatred; two members of the group Pussy Riot were jailed under the provisions of the same law in 2012. For accounts and discussion see Brooks, and Elder.

15. The twenty-first-century reluctance in much of the western world to risk controversy over works of art has not been confined to galleries and museums; it has also become common in other areas of the art world. Art education is an important case in point. In theory, art educators have a great deal of freedom to share and discuss controversial work with their students. In practice, as David Darts has shown, in many jurisdictions "the threat of termination or worse [is] a very real possibility for art teachers who stray from ultra-conservative curricula, or who engage in the production of potentially controversial artwork" (115).

One highly controversial incident that received considerable coverage in Canada occurred in Calgary, Alberta, in 2013. A student at the Alberta College of Art and Design brought a live chicken into the college cafeteria and proceeded to cut off her head, drain the blood, and wash and pluck the bird, all as part of a performance art project intended by the artist to draw attention to "the connection between animals and the food we eat" (qtd. in Schmidt). The project had been approved in advance by an ACAD faculty member; police interviewed the student and the faculty member and declined to press charges under animal cruelty legislation. Three weeks after the incident occurred, however, the college fired the professor who had given his student the go-ahead on the project. For more on the controversy see the articles by Samantha Escobar, Manisha Krishnan, Colleen Schmidt, and Sherri Zickenfoose.

Davis 23

Works Cited

Associated Press. "Bush Backs Giuliani on Museum Flap." *Washington*
　　Post, 4 Oct. 1999, www.washingtonpost.com/wp-srv/
　　aponline/19991004/aponline163720_000.htm. Accessed 20
　　May 2015.

Baker, Kenneth. "Show's Cancellation a Rare Case of Artists
　　Advocating Censorship." *San Francisco Chronicle*, 1 Apr. 2008,
　　p. E1.

Barbaro, Michael. "For Mayoral Hopeful Who Lost Fight to Remove
　　Art, No Regrets." *New York Times*, 27 March 2013,
　　www.nytimes.com/2013/03/28/nyregion/for-lhota-mayoral-
　　hopeful-who-lost-fight-to-remove-art-no-regrets.html?_r=0.
　　Accessed 14 May 2015.

Barry, Dan, and Carol Vogel. "Giuliani Vows to Cut Subsidy over Art
　　He Calls Offensive." *New York Times*, 23 Sept. 1999,
　　partners.nytimes.com/library/arts/092399brooklyn-museum-
　　funds.html. Accessed 20 May 2015.

Blatchford, Christie. "Face to Face with Cruelty." *Globe and Mail*, 4
　　Sept. 2004, p. A13.

Brooklyn Institute of Arts and Sciences v. City of New York 99CV
　　6071. *National Coalition Against Censorship*, 1 Nov. 1999,

each entry begins at left margin; subsequent lines are indented

MLA Sample Essay

works cited are listed alphabetically

Davis 24

ncac.org/resource/brooklyn-institute-of-arts-and-sciences-v-city-
of-new-york. Accessed 2 May 2015.

Brooks, Katherine. "Russia's Hermitage Museum Under Investigation For 'Blasphemous' Jake and Dinos Chapman Exhibit."
Huffington Post, 11 Dec. 2012, www.huffingtonpost.com/2012/
12/11/hermitage-museum-blasphemy-investigation-jake-and-
dinos-chapman_n_2272987.html. Accessed 3 May 2015.

Bruce, Tammy. *The Death of Right and Wrong*. Three Rivers Press,
2003.

Catholic League. "Piss-Christ Coming to New York." *Catholic
League for Civil and Religious Rights*, 21 Sept. 2012,
www.catholicleague.org/piss-christ-coming-to-nyc/. Accessed
19 May 2015.

Cramer, Peter. "Sick Stuff: A Case Study of Controversy in a
Constitutive Attitude." *Rhetoric Society Quarterly*, vol. 43,
no. 2, 2013, pp. 177–201. Taylor & Francis Online, DOI:
10.1080/02773945.2013.768352. Accessed 21 May 2015.

Danto, Arthur C. "'Sensation' in Brooklyn." *The Nation,* 1 Nov. 1999,
www.thenation.com/article/sensation-brooklyn/. Accessed 4
May 2015.

Darts, David. "The Art of Culture War: (Un)Popular Culture,
Freedom of Expression, and Art Education." *Studies in Art*

double
spacing
used
throughout

MLA Sample Essay

italics used
for titles
of books,
journals,
magazines,
etc.

Education, vol. 49, no. 2, Winter 2008, pp. 103–21. JSTOR, www.jstor.org/stable/25475862. Accessed 3 May 2015.

DeBare, Ilana. "Art Institute Halts Exhibition Showing Killing of Animals. " *San Francisco Chronicle,* 30 Mar. 2008, p. B1.

Elder, Miriam. "Russian Museum Could Be Prosecuted over Chapman Brothers Exhibit." *The Guardian*, 7 Dec. 2012, www.theguardian.com/ world/2012/dec/07/russian-museum-chapman-brothers. Accessed 3 May 2013.

Escobar, Samantha. "Professor Fired after Student Kills Chicken in School Cafeteria as 'Performance Art.'" *Blisstree,* 18 Apr. 2013, www.blisstree.com/2013/05/14/food/professor-fired-after-student-kills-chicken-at-school-as-art/. Accessed 19 May 2015.

Hoban, Phoebe. "How Far Is Too Far?" *ArtNews,* Summer 2008, pp. 145–49.

Kekes, John. *A Case for Conservatism.* Ithaca, Cornell UP, 1988.

Kimmelman, Michael. "A Madonna's Many Meanings in the Art World." *New York Times,* 5 Oct. 1999, www.nytimes.com/ 1999/10/05/arts/critic-s-notebook-a-madonna-s-many-meanings-in-the-art-world.html. Accessed 20 May 2015.

Krishnan, Manisha. "Calgary Art Student Kills Chicken in College Cafeteria." *Macleans,* 19 April 2013, www.macleans.ca/ education/uniandcollege/calgary-art-student-kills-chicken-in-college-cafeteria/. Accessed 21 May 2015.

Levine, Peter. "Lessons from the Brooklyn Museum Controversy."
    Philosophy and Public Policy Quarterly, vol. 20, no. 2/3, Summer,
    2000, pp. 19–27.

MacDonald, Gayle. "TIFF Contacts Police over Death Threat: Caller
    Threatens Programmer over Cat-Killer Documentary." *Globe and
    Mail*, 1 Sept. 2004, p. R1.

MacRitchie, Lynn. "Ofili's Glittering Icons." *Art in America*, Jan. 2000,
    pp. 96–101.

Mincheva, Svetlana. "Symbols into Soldiers: Art, Censorship, and
    Religion." *Artsfreedom*, 19 Oct. 2012, artsfreedom.org/?p=3358.
    Accessed 2 May 2015.

Nagourney, Adam. "First Lady Assails Mayor over Threat to
    Museum." *New York Times*, 28 Sept. 1999, www.nytimes.com/
    1999 /09/28/nyregion/first-lady-assails-mayor-over-threat-to-
    museum.html. Accessed 20 May 2015.

Reich, Robert B. *Reason: Why Liberals Will Win the Battle for America.*
    Knopf, 2004.

Rosenbaum, Lee. "The Battle of Brooklyn Ends, the Controversy
    Continues." *Art in America*, June 2000, pp. 39–43.

Rosenberg, Lela Capri. "The Meaning of Sensation: Young British Art
    in the Nineties." Duke University, 2008. ProQuest,

Davis 27

search.proquest.com/docview/304639236?accountid=9838.

Accessed 20 Feb. 2015. Dissertation.

Schlafly, Phyllis. "Time to Abolish Federally Financed 'Hate Art.'"
Eagle Forum, 13 Oct. 1999, www.eagleforum.org/column/1999/
oct99/99-10-13.html. Accessed May 2015.

Schmidt, Colleen. "No Charges in Chicken Killing at ACAD." CTV
Calgary News, 19 April 2013, calgary.ctvnews.ca/no-charges-in-
chicken-killing-at-acad-1.1245321. Accessed 10 Jan. 2015.

"Sensation: Young British Artists from the Saatchi Collection."
Brooklyn Museum, 2 October 1999 to 9 January 2000,
www.brooklynmuseum.org/opencollection/exhibitions/683.
Exhibition.

Smith, Roberta. "Medium and Message, Both Unsettling." Rev. of
Chris Ofili: Night and Day. New Museum, New York. *New
York Times*, 30 Oct. 2014, www.nytimes.com/2014/10/31/
arts/design/chris-ofili-night-and-day-a-survey-at-the-new-
museum.html. Accessed 29 May 2015.

Tomkins, Calvin. "Into the Unknown: Chris Ofili Returns to New
York with a Major Retrospective." *New Yorker*, 6 Oct. 2014,
www.newyorker.com/magazine/2014/10/06/unknown-.

"Turner Prize: Year By Year." *Tate Britain*. www.tate.org.uk/visit/tate-
britain/turner-prize/year-by-year. Accessed 12 May 2015.

Vogel, Carol. "Chris Ofili: British Artist Holds Fast to His Inspir-
 ation." *New York Times,* 28 Sept. 1999, partners.nytimes.com/
 library/arts/092899ofili-brooklyn-museum.html. Accessed 20
 May 2015.

Zickenfoose, Sherri. "Public Slaughter of Chicken Defended as Art."
 Calgary Herald, 18 April 2013, www.calgaryherald.com/public+
 slaughter+chicken+defended/8263036/story.html. Accessed 10
 May 2015.

◎ Sample Essay (APA Style)

top
right-hand
corner
pagination
begins with
title page

Resistance to Vaccination:

A Review of the Literature

Jeremy Yap

Vancouver Island University

author's
name may
appear
either just
below the
title (as
shown)

or at the
bottom
of the
page with
course and
instructor
information

Author note

This paper was prepared for Psychology 230,

taught by Professor J.B. Martin.

Abstract

In the past generation concern over the safety of vaccination against a variety of diseases has become common in North America, as well as in Britain and some other European countries. This paper reviews findings as to the safety of vaccines, as well as of their effectiveness in preventing the diseases they are designed to combat. It also explores the reasons for the now-widespread mistrust of vaccination, looking at the role played by the media, by health care professionals—and looking too at the findings of social psychologists. Finally, it asks what approaches may be most effective in increasing rates of vaccination; in all likelihood, the paper suggests, no single approach is likely to be enough.

separate
page
for the
abstract

APA Sample Essay

Resistance to Vaccination: title should

A Review of the Literature   be centred

Since the late 1990s, vaccination has become highly controversial. This paper will review the literature on the subject, with a particular focus on the vaccination of children, by posing and responding to three key questions:

1.   How effective is the practice of vaccination—and how safe?

2.   Why have vaccination rates declined?

3.   What are the best ways to increase rates of vaccination?

This is an area in which medical science must engage with the research findings of social psychologists; there is an urgent need to find effective solutions. The problems are sufficiently complex, however, that it seems unlikely that any single approach will be sufficient to resolve them.

How Effective Is the Practice of Vaccination—and How Safe?

There is overwhelming evidence on a variety of fronts that vaccination is one of the great triumphs of modern medical science. Thanks to the spread of vaccination, smallpox and polio have been eliminated in most of the world. The Centers for Disease Control and Prevention (2014) reports that diseases such as measles, mumps, and rubella, for which a combined vaccine has for generations been routinely given to children, are almost unknown in areas where vaccination is near-universal. The example of measles is an instructive

APA Sample Essay

one. Before the practice of vaccination was introduced, measles infected several million children every year in the United States alone, and killed more than 500 annually. After vaccination became common practice, measles almost entirely disappeared in North America—until recently. Now it is a threat once again in the United States and Canada—and not a threat to be taken lightly. According to the World Health Organization (2015), measles still kills over 100,000 worldwide each year; for 2012 the figure was 122,000.

for citation of work with six or more authors use "et al."

Evidence for the effectiveness of vaccination is very strong in the case of polio and smallpox, and in the case of "childhood diseases" such as measles and rubella. There is also strong evidence that vaccination against influenza has been successful in bringing about significantly reduced rates of infection (Brewer et al., 2007). Importantly, though, the success of vaccination depends in large part on so-called "herd immunity." So long as approximately 95% or thereabouts of a population have been vaccinated, the incidence of a disease catching on in that population are negligible. When vaccination rates dip below that level, however, the risk for those who have not been vaccinated increases dramatically. Despite this, some communities where vaccination is readily available nonetheless have vaccination rates dramatically below the percentage required for herd immunity. In California, for example, where a 2015 outbreak of measles has received

APA Sample Essay

RESISTANCE TO VACCINATION   5

wide attention, Maimuna et al. (2015) have estimated that in the relevant population clusters vaccination rates have dropped below 50%.

What about the other side of the ledger? Have there been cases of patients suffering adverse effects after taking a vaccine? And if so, do the benefits of vaccination outweigh the risks? Here too the answers seem clear. Yes, there have been cases of adverse effects (notably, fever and allergic reactions for some individuals). But as Bonhoeffer (2007) and others have concluded, these are rare, and on balance vastly outweighed by the benefits of mass vaccination. Perhaps the broadest study of vaccines, their effectiveness, and their occasional side effects was that conducted by the Institute of Medicine (2011), which reviewed vaccines used against chickenpox, influenza, hepatitis B, human papillomavirus, measles, mumps, rubella, meningitis, and tetanus. Their conclusion was clear:

> Vaccines offer the promise of protection against a variety of infectious diseases ... [and] remain one of the greatest tools in the public health arsenal. Certainly, some vaccines result in adverse effects that must be acknowledged. But the latest evidence shows that few adverse effects are caused by the vaccines reviewed in this report. (p. 4)

square brackets used for a word not in the original quotation

Except in rare cases, then (as with certain individuals susceptible to severe allergic reactions), the benefits of vaccines clearly far outweigh the risks.

centred head- ings for sections

Why Have Vaccination Rates Declined?

Near the end of the last century, British medical researcher Andrew Wakefield and his colleagues (1998) published a study linking the vaccination of children against diseases such as measles, mumps, and rubella to increased incidence of gastrointestinal disease, and also to increased incidence of "developmental regression"—notably, autism. The study appeared in *The Lancet*, one of the world's leading medical journals, and had a major impact—but an entirely unfortunate one. News of the study's findings spread widely, with thousands of articles in the popular press in 2001 and 2002 questioning the safety of vaccination. Parents whose children suffered from autism started to blame vaccination, and many of them launched lawsuits.

It was not until six years later that serious doubts were publicly raised. Investigative journalist Brian Deer (2004) revealed that Wakefield's study was compromised by a serious conflict of interest; he had received financial compensation from parties intending to sue vaccine manufacturers before he embarked on the research. And, as was gradually discovered, the research itself had been fabricated. In 2010 *The Lancet* finally retracted the 1998 article, and Wakefield himself was censured. By that time, a very great deal of damage had been done; public confidence in vaccines had dropped precipitously.

APA Sample Essay

Fabricated research results are not the sole cause of the lack of confidence in vaccination that many continue to express. To some extent, confidence in vaccination among the general public has always been shaky. The very nature of vaccination—giving the patient a very small, modified dose of an illness in order to prevent further harm—seems counterintuitive to many. As Brendan Nyhan observed in an interview with Julia Belluz (2015), "people have always been suspicious of vaccines. There has always been an instinctive response to the idea of using a disease to protect yourself against the disease. It gives people the heebie jeebies" (para. 8). In a meta-analysis, Brewer et al. (2007) report that humans are far more likely to get vaccinated when they believe the disease in question to pose a serious threat—a finding which should not come as surprising, and which explains why doubts about vaccines have found fertile ground in places where the vaccines themselves have largely or entirely succeeded. As Jerome Groopman (2015) has observed, "we no longer see children stricken with polio in wheelchairs, or hear of those suffocating from diphtheria, of babies born to mothers with rubella whose eyes are clouded by cataracts and hearts deformed" (p. 30). If one continually sees people suffering from such diseases, one is likely to be far more aware of their dangers than is the case in nations where vaccination has succeeded in reducing their incidence to zero or near-zero.

running head may either be in caps (as shown) or upper and lower case

APA Sample Essay

When doubts have been raised and scandals have arisen, the media have too often not been as responsible as one would wish. On the one hand, as discussed by Nelson (2014), Mooney (2011) and others, some media outlets have tacitly encouraged scientifically irresponsible statements by taking an "impartial" approach to the facts, reporting the claims of anti-vaccination activists with no scientific credentials and of reputable scientific authorities as if they had equal authority. Other media outlets, however, have sometimes swung too far in the other direction, adopting a supercilious or contemptuous tone towards those who have doubts about vaccination. Much as it is important to spread factual information as to the dangers of allowing one's children to remain unvaccinated, it is counterproductive to present information in a tone that is disrespectful of the audience one is hoping to persuade. As Angelina Chapin (2015) has pointed out, when

accept-
able to
include
first
name in
a signal
phrase

> people's beliefs contradict science, there's an obvious temptation to cut them down. But we should be more careful with how we deliver our arguments. On a policy level, messaging should come from people that communities trust, such as doctors or religious leaders. At the dinner table or on Facebook, try a little empathy. It will help the medicine go down and the immunization rates go up. (para. 12)

AIA Sample Essay

The attitudes with which we approach these discussions, in short, can make a world of difference.

Interestingly, studies such as that of Maimuna et al. (2015) suggest that those with high levels of education are at least as likely as those with less education to be anti-vaccination. One important factor in the social psychology of attitudes towards vaccination that does seem to have had an impact (albeit a negative one), has been the degree to which the issue has become charged with ideological content. Those who are generally suspicious of government and/or of modern science have been slow to accept the overwhelming weight of evidence in support of vaccination. That should perhaps not be surprising; as Kraft, Lodge, and Taber (2015) and others have reported, to the extent that beliefs about factual matters are intertwined with ideology, our minds become immunized against information in the other direction, even when that information is of a purely factual nature. Moreover, this is a "tendency that appears to be evident among liberals and conservatives alike" (p. 121). When they are coloured by ideology—and by emotion—our beliefs as to the facts of the matter are highly resistant to change.

in signal phrase, "and" used to link author names

What Are the Best Ways to Increase the Rates of Vaccination?

Clearly it is important for health care workers, educators, and those in the media to inform themselves of the facts and to spread this

APA Sample Essay

information. But simply informing the public of the facts is evidently insufficient to change behaviour. Several studies have found that parents who have been fully informed of the scientific background are no more likely to vaccinate their children—and in some cases are *less* likely (Nyhan, Reifler, Richey, & Freed, 2014; Mills, Jadadc, Ross, & Wilson, 2005).

in paren-
thetical
citation,
amper-
sand (not
"and")
used
to link
author
names

Just important as the facts themselves, it seems, is the way they are reported to patients. The attitudes expressed by health care workers to patients play a key role. Though the vast majority of health care workers accept the evidence regarding vaccination, they have become aware that it is a hot-button issue and—not wanting to be insensitive to patients' concerns—have sometimes not been clear and emphatic about the dangers of not vaccinating. If health care workers ask parents if they "believe in" vaccinating their children, their phrasing is likely to provide support to the views of those patients who think the science about vaccinations to be uncertain. Conversely, an attitude that remains friendly while taking the facts as a given may be more helpful. There have been numerous studies on the degree to which it may help to frame information positively to patients (Marsh, Malik, Shapiro, & Omer, 2014; Wegwartha, Kurzenhäuser-Carstens, & Gigerenzera, 2014; and O'Keefea & Xiaoli, 2012). Though these have not been entirely conclusive, it is hard to imagine that it is not preferable to present facts in a tone that will encourage others to appreciate them, and to act accordingly. Angelina Chapin's common-sense advice on this point (quoted above) rings true.

It may well be, however, that adopting the right tone with patients and in media reports will not be enough; regulatory and/or legislative changes may be required as well in some jurisdictions. It is important to note that the United States as a whole has not suffered any steep decline in vaccination rates; to a large extent the problem is associated with jurisdictions that make it easy for parents to opt out of vaccinations for their children. In contrast, where vaccination is the strong "default position"—mandatory for children with few possible exemptions—vaccination rates in recent years have tended to remain at well over 90%. As Margaret Talbot (2015) has observed of the United States,

> the highest vaccination rate in the country is in
> Mississippi, a state with an otherwise dismal set of
> health statistics. It allows people to opt out of vaccines
> only for medical reasons—not for religious or personal ones.
> States that make it easier not to vaccinate have
> higher rates of infectious diseases. (pp. 19–20)

Is the answer, then, simply to pass stricter laws in jurisdictions that currently have loose ones? Much as such action may be desirable, given

quotation of more than 40 words is indented

APA Sample Essay

current levels of resistance to vaccination of children, it is questionable
whether efforts to make the practice mandatory would be successful
in many areas—and they would be sure to inflame passions on all sides.

The experience of the European Union suggests that it may not
always be necessary to make vaccination mandatory. Vaccination rates
are high throughout Europe, even though only 14 of the 29 countries
in the EU have any mandatory vaccinations (Haverkate et al., 2012).
In the remainder, vaccination is recommended rather than required.
There is some evidence that in North America, too, non-compulsory
strategies can in certain circumstances be as effective as compulsion
in raising vaccination rates (El-Amin, Parra, Kim-Farley, & Fielding,
2012). Again, the strength with which a recommendation is put
forward can make a world of difference to the degree to which that
recommendation is followed. If parents are simply informed that
vaccination is recommended and that they may vaccinate their children
against measles if they wish at such and such a time and place, the
uptake rate is likely to be low. If parents are informed that a medical
ordinance specifies that children should be vaccinated against measles,
and that low vaccination rates put all children at risk, the uptake rate
will surely be much higher.

There is a widespread tendency to presume that Americans will
be more likely to resist government "intrusions" into citizen's lives than

will Canadians. In the case of attitudes towards vaccination, however, it is not at all clear that the presumption is correct. Whereas every American state has at least some requirement (albeit often weakened by "personal belief" exemptions) that children be vaccinated before attending school, only a minority of Canadian provinces have such regulations (Walkinshaw, 2011).

Whatever approaches are taken in each jurisdiction, it will be essential that attention be paid not only to the medical and biological facts, but also to laws and regulations—and to social psychology.

list of references begins on a new page

References

Belluz, J. (2015, February 7). Debunking vaccine junk science won't change people's minds. Here's what will. [Interview with B. Nyhan]. *Vox*. Retrieved from http://www.vox .com/2015/2/7/7993289/vaccine-beliefs

Bonhoeffer J., & Heininger U. (2007). Adverse events following immunization: perception and evidence. *Current Opinion in Infectious Diseases, 20*(3), 237–246. doi:10.1097 /QCO.0b013e32811ebfb0

Brewer, N. T., Chapman, G. B., Gibbons, F. X., Gerrard, M., McCaul, K. D., & Weinstein, N. D. (2007). Meta-analysis of the relationship between risk perception and health behaviour: The example of vaccination. *Health Psychology, 26*(2), 136–145. doi:10.1037/0278-6133.26.2.136

Chapin, A. (2015, February 13). How to talk to anti-vaxxers. *Ottawa Citizen*. Retrieved from http://ottawacitizen.com/opinion /columnists/how-to-talk-to-anti-vaxxers

Deer, B. (2004, February 22). Revealed: MMR research scandal. *The Sunday Times* (London). Retrieved from http://www .thesundaytimes.co.uk/sto/

El-Amin, A. N., Parra, M.T., Kim-Farley, R., & Fielding, J.E. (2012). Ethical issues concerning vaccination requirements. *Public Health*

list of references alphabetized by author's last name

author initials used—not first names

Reviews, 34(1), 1–20. Retrieved from http://www
.publichealthreviews.eu/upload/pdf_files/11/00_El_Amin.pdf

Groopman, J. (2015, March 5). There's no way out of it. [Review of
the book *On immunity: An introduction*]. *The New York Review of
Books*, 29–31.

Haverkate, M., D'Ancona, F., Giambi, C., Johansen, K., Lopalco, P.
L., Cozza, V., & Appelgren, E. (2012, May). Mandatory and
recommended vaccination in the EU, Iceland and Norway:
results of the VENICE 2010 survey on the ways of implementing
national vaccination programmes. *Eurosurveillance, 17*(22), 31.
Retrieved from http://www.eurosurveillance.org/ViewArticle
.aspx?ArticleId=20183

Institute of Medicine. (2011, August 25). Adverse effects of vaccines:
Evidence and causality. Report brief. Retrieved from http://www
.iom.edu/Reports/2011/Adverse-Effects-of-Vaccines-Evidence
-and-Causality.aspx

Kraft, P. W., Lodge, M., & Taber, C. S. (2015, March). Why people
"don't trust the evidence": Motivated reasoning and scientific
beliefs. *Annals of the American Academy of Political and Social
Science, 658*(1), 121–133. doi:10.1177/0002716214554758

Maimuna, S., Majumder, M. P. H., Cohn, E. L., Sumiko, R., Mekaru,
D. V. M., Huston, J. E., & Brownstein, J. S. (2015, March

for web-
accessed
material
provide
DOI
whenever
available

16). Substandard vaccination compliance and the 2015 measles outbreak. *JAMA Pediatrics.* doi:10.1001/jamapediatrics .2015.0384

Marsh, H.A., Malik, F., Shapiro, E., & Omer, S.B. (2014, September). Message framing strategies to increase influenza immunization uptake among pregnant African American women. *Maternal and Child Health Journal, 18*(7), 1639–1647. doi:10.1007 /s10995-013-1404-9

Measles History (2014, November 3). Center for Disease Control and Prevention website. Retrieved from http://www.cdc.gov /measles/about/history.html

Mills, E., Jadadc, A. R., Ross, C., & Wilson, K. (2005, November). Systematic review of qualitative studies exploring parental beliefs and attitudes toward childhood vaccination identifies common barriers to vaccination. *Journal of Clinical Epidemiology, 58*(11), 1081–1088. doi:http://dx.doi.org/10.1016/j .jclinepi.2005.09.002

Mooney, C. (2011, May/June). The science of why we don't believe science. *Mother Jones.* Retrieved from http://www.motherjones .com/politics/2011/03/denial-science-chris-mooney

Nelson, R. (2014, October). The reporting of health information in the media. *American Journal of Nursing, 114*(10), 19–20.

doi:10.1097/01.NAJ.0000454842.04985.c6

Nyhan, B. (2013, July 16). When "he said, she said" is dangerous. *Columbia Journalism Review*. Retrieved from http://www.cjr.org /united_states_project/media_errs_giving_balanced_coverage _to_jenny_mccarthys_discredited_views.php

Nyhan, B., Reifler, J., Richey, S., & Freed, G.L. (2014, April 1). Effective messages in vaccine promotion: A randomized trial. *Pediatrics, 133*(4), e835–e842. doi:10.1542/peds.2013-2365

O'Keefea, D. J., & Xiaoli, N. (2012). The relative persuasiveness of gain- and loss-framed messages for promoting vaccination: A meta-analytic review. *Health Communication, 27*(8), 776–783. doi :10.1080/10410236.2011.640974

Talbot, M. (2015, February 16). Not immune. *The New Yorker, 91*(1), 19–20.

Wakefield, A.J., Murch, S.H., Anthony, A., Linnel, J., Casson, D.M., Malik, M., … Walker-Smith, J.A. (1998). Ileal-lymphoid-nodular hyperplasia, non-specific colitis, and pervasive developmental disorder in children. *Lancet, 351*, 637–641. (Retraction published 2010, *Lancet, 375*, p. 445)

Walkinshaw, E. (2011, November 8). Mandatory vaccinations: The international landscape. *Canadian Medical Association Journal, 183*(16), e1167–e1168. doi:10.1503/cmaj.109-3993

provide URL for web-sourced material when DOI not available

Wegwartha, O., Kurzenhäuser-Carstens, S., & Gigerenzera, G.
(2014, March 10). Overcoming the knowledge–behaviour
gap: The effect of evidence-based HPV vaccination leaflets on
understanding, intention, and actual vaccination decision.
Science Direct: Vaccine, 32(12), 1388–1393. doi:10.1016
/j.vaccine.2013.12.038

World Health Organization (n.d.). Measles (Immunization, Vaccines
and Biologicals). World Health Organization website.
Retrieved from http://www.who.int/immunization
/monitoring_surveillance/burden/vpd/surveillance_type/active
/measles/en/

From the Publisher

A name never says it all, but the word "Broadview" expresses a good deal of the philosophy behind our company. We are open to a broad range of academic approaches and political viewpoints. We pay attention to the broad impact book publishing and book printing has in the wider world; we began using recycled stock more than a decade ago, and for some years now we have used 100% recycled paper for most titles. Our publishing program is internationally oriented and broad-ranging. Our individual titles often appeal to a broad readership too; many are of interest as much to general readers as to academics and students.

Founded in 1985, Broadview remains a fully independent company owned by its shareholders—not an imprint or subsidiary of a larger multinational.

For the most accurate information on our books (including information on pricing, editions, and formats) please visit our website at www.broadviewpress. com. Our print books and ebooks are also available for sale on our site.

On the Broadview website we also offer several goods that are not books— among them the Broadview coffee mug, the Broadview beer stein (inscribed with a line from Geoffrey Chaucer's *Canterbury Tales*), the Broadview fridge magnets (your choice of philosophical or literary), and a range of T-shirts (made from combinations of hemp, bamboo, and/or high-quality pima cotton, with no child labor, sweatshop labor, or environmental degradation involved in their manufacture).

All these goods are available through the "merchandise" section of the Broadview website. When you buy Broadview goods you can support other goods too.

broadview press
www.broadviewpress.com